"YOU'VE HEARD IT SAID"

Other Books by Gary DeMar

God and Government: A Biblical and Historical Study, 1990

God and Government: Issues in Biblical Perspective, 1990

God and Government: The Restoration of the Republic, 1990

Ruler of the Nations, 1987

Surviving College Successfully, 1988

The Reduction of Christianity: A Biblical Response to Dave Hunt (with Peter Leithart), 1988

Something Greater Is Here, 1988

The Debate over Christian Reconstruction, 1988

The Legacy of Hatred Continues (with Peter Leithart), 1989

Gary DeMar (signature)

GARY DeMAR

"YOU'VE HEARD IT SAID"

15 BIBLICAL MISCONCEPTIONS THAT
RENDER CHRISTIANS POWERLESS

Wolgemuth & Hyatt, Publishers, Inc.
Brentwood, Tennessee

137578

The mission of Wolgemuth & Hyatt, Publishers, Inc. is to publish and distribute books that lead individuals toward:

- A personal faith in the one true God: Father, Son, and Holy Spirit;

- A lifestyle of practical discipleship; and

- A worldview that is consistent with the historic, Christian faith.

Moreover, the Company endeavors to accomplish this mission at a reasonable profit and in a manner which glorifies God and serves His Kingdom.

Unless otherwise noted, all Scripture quotations are from the New American Standard Bible, ©1960, 1962, 1963, 1968, 1971, 1972, 1973, 1975, 1977, by The Lockman Foundation and are used by permission.

Wolgemuth & Hyatt, Publishers, Inc.
1749 Mallory Lane, Suite 110
Brentwood, Tennessee 37027

Library of Congress Cataloging-in-Publication Data

DeMar, Gary.
  You've heard it said : 15 biblical misinterpretations that render
Christians powerless / Gary DeMar.—1st ed.
      p. cm.
  Includes bibliographical references.
  ISBN 1-56121-049-8
  1. Church and the world. 2. Church and social problems.
3. Christianity and politics. 4. Eschatology. I. Title.
BR115.W6D42 1991
261—dc20
                                        91-6447
                                           CIP

Dedicated to the memory of G. Aiken Taylor
(1920–1984)

CONTENTS

INTRODUCTION

*Have nothing to do with worldly fables fit
only for old women.*

1 TIMOTHY 4:7a

I n recent years a number of books have been published designed to give a more accurate interpretation of history and to demolish long-held myths. For example, one of the most cherished historical myths is that Christopher Columbus sailed west from Europe to prove that the world was round.[1] Columbus's biographer, Eliot Morison, describes the story as "pure moonshine" and "misleading and mischievous nonsense."[2]

The Pythagoreans of the sixth century B.C. taught that the world was spherical, and Aristotle proved it by observing "during an eclipse that the earth casts a spherical shadow on the moon."[3] The scientists and church leaders of the sixteenth century taught that the earth was round based on a study of the created order and Scripture:

> Scientific demonstration of the earth's rotundity was enforced by religion; God made the earth a sphere because that was the most perfect form. In the Old Testament there is a reference to this in Isaiah xl.22: "It is he that sitteth upon the circle of the earth"—"circle" being the translation of the Hebrew *khug*, sphere.[4]

In the year Columbus sailed into history, Martin Behaim of Nuremberg, Germany, produced a terrestrial globe. You don't make a globe if you believe the earth is flat.

Deep and Wide

The debate in Columbus's day was not whether the earth was flat or round. "The issue was the width of the ocean; and therein the opposition was right."[5] Columbus had underestimated the circumference of the earth and the width of the ocean by a significant number of miles. Providentially, the Americas stood in his way and shortened what would have been an otherwise very long and nearly impossible voyage:

> Educated opinion in Columbus's day was that the earth was a sphere of about 24,000 miles in circumference. Therefore, since China was some 8,000 miles to the east, the conventional wisdom held it impractical to sail west for 16,000 miles to reach the Orient. That is why Columbus had such a hard time finding backers for his concept.
>
> Columbus calculated the earth's circumference at about 18,000 miles, and he also believed Ptolemy's too-large estimate of the eastward extent of Asia. Combining these two errors, he came to the conclusion Japan lay about 3,000 miles to the west of the Canary Islands.[6]

Columbus made additional mistakes. He believed the length of a degree to be 56.66 miles, when actually its correct value is nearly 69 statute miles at the equator. It's possible that if Columbus had been correctly informed on the earth's circumference and the length of a degree, he might have stayed home! Ptolemy's mistaken calculations were "a happy mistake. For it encouraged navigators like Columbus and Cabot to believe that the Atlantic could be crossed in a reasonable time."[7]

Cherished Biblical Myths

While the myths surrounding Columbus's navigational exploits are interesting, there is nothing in these myths that has a direct impact on the Christian's walk with Jesus Christ. There are, however, lessons to be learned from our brief study of Columbus and the flat-earth myth and certain cherished myths about the Bible. Numerous biblical myths plague the church. Some of these myths are harmless since they do not affect our salvation: the belief that the forbidden fruit was an apple (no fruit is specified), that Jonah was swallowed by a whale (it was "a great fish"), and that angels have wings (they don't), for example. There are other myths that parade as facts, only because we have heard them for

---

"Numerous biblical myths plague the church."

---

so long and fail to examine "the Scriptures daily, to see whether these things were so" (Acts 17:11).

When asked, "Who cut off Samson's hair?" the typical response is, "Delilah." But a close look at the biblical text will show that Delilah "called for a man and had him shave off the seven locks of his hair."

> And she had made him sleep on her knees, and *called for a man and had him shave off the seven locks of his hair*. Then she began to afflict him, and his strength left him. (Judges 16:19, emphasis added)

While the Samson and Delilah hair removal story is not a central doctrine of the Christian faith, it does demonstrate that if a myth is passed on with few people ever checking the facts, then the myth becomes a fact by default.

Even the absence or the presence of a word is important. How many of you have been told, and now believe, that Jesus, as He prayed in the Garden of Gethsemane, "sweat great drops of blood"? What does Scripture say?

> And being in agony He was praying very fervently; and His sweat became *like* drops of blood, falling down upon the ground. (Luke 22:44, emphasis added)

There is a big difference in sweating "drops of blood" and "His sweat became *like* drops of blood." All the student of Scripture has to do to expose myths such as these is to open his or her Bible and read. Take, for example, the use of *leaven* in Scripture. Some interpreters maintain that the word *leaven* always symbolizes evil. Is this true? A study of the word and its usage in various contexts will demonstrate

that leaven does not always symbolize evil. How do I know? Look up
every reference to *leaven* in a concordance and see for yourself. There
are at least two places where the use of leaven symbolizes something
good. How about the word *serpent*? Is the word *serpent* always a symbol
for evil? No! (You will have to read this book to find the answer to the
serpent question.)

Take the following test, and see how well you do. The answers are
found in the endnotes:

1. Is Mount Ararat the resting place for Noah's Ark? (Genesis
   8:4).[8]
2. Where does the phrase "ashes to ashes, dust to dust" appear in
   Scripture?[9]
3. Does Scripture say that Jesus was crucified at a place called
   "Calvary"? (Matthew 27:33; Mark 15:22; Luke 23:33; John
   19:17).[10]
4. Where did the wise men pay homage to the child Jesus?[11]

Again, a belief in these "myths," like the belief in the Columbus
myth, has little overt effect on the average Christian. There is, however, an underlying danger. If Christians have adopted myths as truths
in areas where little if any interpretation is needed, is it possible that
they may have adopted myths as truths in areas where greater study is
needed?

You've Heard It Said

Jesus encountered similar misunderstanding during His short three-year
earthly ministry. He dealt with the problem head on: "You have heard
that the ancients were told. . . ." (Matthew 5:21) and "You have heard
that it was said. . . ." (v. 27) were repeated by Jesus five times in a series
of twenty-eight verses. If we were to translate Jesus' words using today's
contemporary usage, we might hear Jesus say: "Contrary to popular
opinion, you are mistaken on what you think the Bible says. You are,
therefore, equally mistaken on how it applies. Let Me clear up the confusion for you by directing you to take a closer look at Scripture." Jesus
was correcting erroneous beliefs about the Bible; He was not rebuking

them for not believing that the Bible was God's infallible and inerrant Word. Jesus' indictment was directed at *believers* who presupposed trustworthiness of Scripture. In His ministry, Jesus touched on four areas:

- An out-of-context reading and application of a text (Matthew 5:21)
- A misreading or an incomplete reading of a text (Matthew 5:38)
- A misstatement of fact (Matthew 5:43)
- Faulty reasoning from an incorrectly established premise (John 9:1–3)

Jesus was not declaring a new set of rules for the church to obey. He was simply holding them responsible to take a closer look at what had been written. For example, if you read Matthew 5:38–40 and com-

---

"Christians should check the veracity of all opinions against the only reliable standard of authority that God has placed in our hands: the Bible."

---

pare it with Exodus 21:22, you will notice that Jesus did not replace capital punishment with a turn-the-other-cheek ethic, thereby establishing a pacifist worldview. Exodus 21:22 clearly states that "judges" are to decide what punishment is to be meted out. Victims could not take personal vengeance (Romans 12:18–21; 13:4). There were some in Jesus' day who took a law that was meant for a civil court and instead applied it in personal relationships without the supervision of the judiciary. Under such conditions, blood feuds often arose. D. A. Carson gives a very helpful interpretation of Jesus' words:

> Jesus says something like this: "You have heard that it was said . . . but I tell you. . . ." He does not begin these contrasts by telling them what the Old Testament said, but what they had heard it said. This is an important observation, because Jesus is not negating something from the Old Testament, but something from their understanding of it.

In other words, Jesus appears to be concerned with two things: overthrowing erroneous traditions, and indicating authoritatively the real direction toward which the Old Testament Scriptures point.[12]

Like the Bereans of Paul's day (Acts 17:11), Christians should check the veracity of all opinions against the only reliable standard of authority that God has placed in our hands: the Bible. This may mean a change in theology for some. This is not new. God had to change the views of Peter regarding the inclusion of the Gentiles into the household of faith (Acts 10:9–16). Paul confronted Peter "to his face" on a similar matter (Galatians 2:11–14). There are times when we all need to be knocked off our theological horses (Acts 9:4) to remind us that God is God, and "we are but dust" (Psalm 103:14).

Contrary to Popular Opinion

This book adopts Jesus' methodology in dealing with theological "rumors" and applies it to certain erroneous traditions that have developed in the church and have resulted in a virtual shut-down of the church's mission in the world (Acts 20:27). These traditional and erroneous interpretations of popular Bible texts and their misapplication to contemporary issues have resulted in the Christian faith being "thrown out and trampled under foot by men" (Matthew 5:13).

There was a time when the gospel of Jesus Christ touched every area of a person's life and the world in which he lived. This is no longer the case. Certainly the humanists have attempted to bar Christ's words from what is often described as the secular realm. But Christians have barred themselves by teaching a one-dimensional gospel: The Bible tells us how to go to heaven, but it does not tell us how the heavens go. We've left that to the humanists. For example, if Christians are so disturbed that the humanists set the cultural agenda, then why do a majority of Christian parents send their children to schools that deny Christ and His Word?

Our nation is in a crisis. The world is crying out for answers in the face of bewildering and seemingly unsolvable problems. This book demonstrates that the Bible has real answers. It also seeks to demonstrate that the church has been instrumental throughout history in the development of what is uniformly described as "civilization." As our nation moves further away from the light of the gospel, we will see only the twilight of our once-Christian civilization.

Neutralized No Longer

To demonstrate the validity of Christianity as a religion for all of life, we need to demythologize the misrepresentations that have been fostered and nurtured by a bewildering number of unorthodox theologies.

"Our nation is in a crisis. The world is crying out for answers in the face of bewildering and seemingly unsolvable problems. . . . The Bible has real answers."

These cherished myths have neutralized the Word of God as it relates to this world:

> Christianity has often been accused of being too "otherworldly" in that it has failed to offer viable political, economic, judicial, and social programs for the world order. The teaching of Jesus that his kingdom "is not of this world" has been interpreted to mean that earthly life must merely be endured, and that Christians cannot expect to accomplish lasting reform before the return of Christ. But does the New Testament really offer no guidance for shaping political or economic policy? Does it contain no judicial or social precepts that may be applied in today's society? True, neither Jesus nor Paul spoke in detail of political or economic ideologies. But since both spoke out of a Jewish background and context, direct allusions may have been unnecessary. Christians must understand that their faith is rooted in Old Testament Judaism and that the Mosaic Covenant and Law (which contain highly specific political, economic, judicial, and social precepts) can give guidance even today. The fact that such ideals exist as

an intrinsic part of Christianity can go a long way toward establishing the credibility of the faith in these areas.[13]

Christianity's failure to be a practical religion in the last eighty years or so has meant the temporary success of a perverted and twisted humanism that has done irreputable harm around the world. Humanism has won by default. The Christian's rejection of any type of this-worldly application of the Bible resulted in the proliferation of a man-centered worldview that steadily drained the life out of our world. Will the church of our Lord Jesus Christ be ready with biblical answers for the millions who will be ready to follow the light of the gospel of grace and all that it means for their lives this side of heaven as the worldview of humanism continues to be exposed as "folly"? (2 Timothy 3:9). Now is the time to make the necessary theological preparations. It is my prayer that this book will help you in that pilgrimage.

PART 1

THE CHRISTIAN
AND THE WORLD

"THE WORLD IS EVIL"

I believe in God the Father Almighty,
Maker of Heaven and Earth.

THE APOSTLES' CREED

D o you realize that the Declaration of Independence bases its doc-trine of "inalienable rights" on the doctrine of creation? The Declaration states simply but essentially that "they are endowed by their Creator with certain inalienable Rights, that among these are Life, Lib-erty and the pursuit of Happiness." No Creator means no inalienable rights. The driving principle of our great nation is that God is the prov-idential ruler of heaven and earth. Even non-Christians like Thomas Jefferson recognized and supported this truth. "And can the liberties of a nation be thought secure when we have removed their only firm basis, a conviction in the minds of the people that these liberties are the gift of God?"

When the belief that God created the heavens and the earth is rejected, as it is in our day, rights soon are extinguished or reinter-preted, so much so that now killing the unborn has become a "right," a direct contradiction of the Declaration of Independence which declares that life is an endowment (gift) from the Creator. "The starting point for a biblical model of rights theory is Genesis 1 and 2. There we find that in the beginning God created the universe. As Creator or Author, God has the inherent right to decide or dispose of all that He has cre-ated. He is sovereign. He is the Lord of all, and He governs all. Of Him and through Him and to Him are all things. The created universe is entirely subject to Him and dependent upon Him in everything."[1]

But there is more to the doctrine of creation than inalienable rights. The doctrine of creation tells us that the created order is the arena for Christian ministry. God put man and woman in the midst of the garden to "cultivate it and keep it" (Genesis 2:15). Rulership was also given to man. While God reserves ultimate rulership for Himself, He delegates a subordinate lordship to man as a steward and vice-regent over the created order. God also sets the rules by which man is to exercise that stewardship. In fact, it was the breaking of these rules that got Adam and Eve exiled from the garden (Genesis 3:22–24).

A good number of Christians have forsaken the doctrine of creation, not as a belief, but as a practical application of a belief. They believe that God created the heavens and the earth, but they fail to recognize the implications of that belief. The created order is considered an encumbrance. The first step in denying God is denying what it means to live in the midst of God's creation. This book deals with numerous misconceptions about the world in which we live and the stewardship that remains because God is still "the maker of heaven and earth."

"Christian! What Do You Believe?"

The Apostles' Creed is recited every Sunday by millions of Protestants and Roman Catholics around the world. How many of these millions have really considered the implications of what they profess? Although not written by the apostles, the Apostles' Creed is an ancient declaration of what the early church believed about the essentials of the Christian faith.

The Doctrine of Creation

The opening line of the Apostles' Creed tells us that God is the "Maker of Heaven and Earth," of a creation that Scripture describes as being "very good" (Genesis 1:31). God is not the world, as in pantheism, nor is He indifferent to the world, as in deism. Neither is the world an emanation from God as in New Age humanism. "The creed confesses a

---

"The first step in denying God is denying what it means to live in the midst of God's creation."

---

living God; no detached spectator on the world and its fate, God is the leading actor. All powerful, he retains and exercises the initiative. This is the most basic theme in the Christian world view."[2]

Sin has certainly affected the world. Although the world is fallen, God has not forsaken the world. His redeeming work in this world has a transforming effect on all aspects of the created order. God was pleased to dwell in Christ "and through Him to reconcile all things to Himself, having made peace through the blood of His cross; through Him, I say, *whether things on earth or things in heaven*" (Colossians 1:20, emphasis added). We learn through Scripture that "whatever is born of God overcomes the world; and this is the victory that has overcome the world—our faith" (1 John 5:4). "The Christian's responsibility on earth is to transform the world that 'thy will be done, on earth as it is in heaven' (Matthew 6:10)."[3]

God is the One who brought "heaven and earth" into existence and "upholds all things by the word of His power" (Hebrews 1:3); this alone should be enough to convince all Christians who recite the opening line to the Apostles' Creed that this world should count for something. While evil may exist in this world because of man's sin, the world in and of itself is not evil. "Whatsoever is evil, is not so by the Creator's action, but by the creature's defection."[4] Therefore, we should be skeptical of any theology that defames any part of God's good creation. "There is no nature originally sinful, no substance in itself evil, no being, therefore, which may not come from the same fountain of goodness."[5]

Supposed Negative Passages

One reason many Christians have shunned involvement in issues beyond personal piety is because a number of passages seem to teach that we should avoid the world and the things of the world, as if *world* is used exclusively for planet Earth rather than referring to a worldview and ethical system that belies the Word of Christ. The world is said to be under God's condemnation (1 Corinthians 11:32). Peter speaks of "the corruption that is in the world" (2 Peter 1:4) and the "defilements of the world" (2:20). From this alone many conclude that any contact with the world (earth) and the things that operate in the world (possessions) will by their very nature affect the Christian's relationship with Jesus Christ.

Since the Bible uses the word *world* in a variety of ways in diverse contexts, we should not take the way *world* is used in one context and assume that it's being used the same way in every context. For example, the word *lion* refers to both Jesus and Satan. The context gives us the proper setting for interpretation. Jesus is the lion from the tribe of Judah (Revelation 5:5), and Satan prowls around like a roaring lion (1 Peter 5:8). If we follow the logic that some use in reference to *world*—that the use of *world* in the Bible is always a description of an evil domain— then we could make a similar claim regarding the use of *lion*, a preposterous idea to be sure.

If the use of a word like *world* always means something evil (which it does not), then what do we do with a word like *serpent*? Satan is depicted as a serpent in several places in Scripture (Genesis 3:1; 2 Corinthians 11:3; Revelation 12:9; 20:2). At the same time, without any qualification, God's people are told to be "shrewd as serpents" (Matthew 10:16). Can we conclude from this that Christians are to be shrewd, evil, like Satan? What about the "fiery serpents" that God sent "so that many people of Israel died"? (Numbers 21:6). Are these serpents evil? If they are, then what about the "fiery serpent" Moses was to make so "that everyone who is bitten, when he looks at it, he shall live"? (v. 8). In one verse (v. 6) the serpent kills. In another verse (v. 9) the serpent saves. To further complicate matters, the bronze serpent is a type of Christ:

"And as Moses lifted up the serpent in the wilderness, even so must the Son of Man be lifted up" (John 3:14):

> Jesus compared His impending crucifixion to the saving event of the days of Moses. Just as the serpent brought deliverance when raised on a pole for all to see, so He, who was made sin for us (2 Corinthians 5:21), would be raised on a cross to deliver mankind from the penalty of wickedness (John 12:32). In the same way that the ancient Israelite was required to look in faith at the bronze serpent to be saved from death, so the modern sinner must also look in faith at the crucified Christ to receive the healing of the new birth (John 3:14–16).[6]

We would end up with a perverted view of salvation if we conclude that the use of the word *serpent* is always a designation of evil. Like

---

"While evil may exist in this world because of man's sin, the world in and of itself is not evil."

---

serpent, the word *world* can have a number of easily understood meanings if the context in which the word appears is taken into consideration.

Many Worlds from Which to Choose

We use the word *world* to describe many different ideas. This is especially true in literature. Few people are able to distinguish the various usages of *world* when they are given the context of the conversation. Here are several examples:

- *Earthly state of human existence*: "God's in his heaven, All's right with the world!"[7]
- *A future state of existence*: "One doth but breakfast here, another dines, he that liveth longest doth but sup; we must all go to be in another world."[8]

- *Posterity:* "The brave men, living and dead, who struggled here, have consecrated it far above our power to add or detract. The world will little note, nor long remember, what we say here, but it can never forget what they did here."[9]

- *The earth or a region:* "My country is the world, and my religion is to do good."[10]

- *Present conditions:* "I, a stranger and afraid in a world I never made."[11]

- *Intensifying an interrogative:* "How, why, what in the world?"

- *A series of seven baseball games:* "The World Series."[12]

- *Planets:* H. G. Wells's *War of the Worlds*.

- *To express uniqueness:* "He's out of this world."

- *To describe oddness:* "He acts like he's from another world."

- *In opposition to everyone:* "He's trying to take on the whole world" (*contra mundum*).

- *A great amount:* "She gave me for my pains a world of kisses [or sighs]."[13]

The Biblical Use of "World"

Since we use *world* in a variety of ways in ordinary speech and literature, we should not be surprised to learn that the Bible also uses *world* in numerous ways. Let's take a brief look at the way the Bible uses the word *world* and then make some determination if it is at all legitimate to be involved in the world.

The world as God's creation (world = created order): "He was in the world, and the world was made through Him. . . ." (John 1:10; Hebrews 1:2–3). *Kosmos,* the Greek word for world, can designate the entire created order (Matthew 13:35; 24:21; 25:34; Luke 11:50; John 17:5, 24) or the earth in particular (Matthew 4:8; 13:38; Mark 14:9; Luke 12:30; John 11:9; 16:21; 21:25). The world was created by Jesus (Colossians 1:16), and the Bible tells us that it is "very good" (Genesis 1:31; 1 Timothy 4:4).

The world as the object of God's redeeming grace (world = comprehensive redemption): "For God so loved the world, that He gave His only begotten Son, that whoever believes in Him should not perish, but have eternal life" (John 3:16; 2 Corinthians 5:19). Typically this verse has been used to teach that Jesus died for every individual in the world. In context, however, we should understand that Jesus' love has no bounds, that it is not restricted to any one group of people. The "eternal gospel" is to be preached "to those who live on the earth, and to every nation and tribe and tongue and people" (Revelation 14:6).

The world as distinct from Judaism (world = non-Jews): "[T]his One is indeed the Savior of the world" [i.e., including Samaritans and later Gentiles] (John 4:42). Similar to the use of *world* described under the previous point, this verse teaches that there will be a great ingrafting of non-Jews into the kingdom. This was recognized early by the Samaritans (John 4:9; Acts 8:25). Prior to Pentecost the gospel was almost exclusively an Israelite gospel, although there were significant exceptions (Matthew 10:5; 15:21-28). A family could be incorporated into Israel by faith (e.g., Rahab's family: Joshua 2:8–14; Matthew 1:5). Under the New Covenant, there is neither Jew nor Gentile (Galatians 3:28) since the dividing wall separating the two worlds—Jewish and Gentile—was dismantled by Christ (Ephesians 2:11–22). But this was an exception rather than the rule prior to the coming of Jesus as the Savior of the world. Jesus' redemptive love extends to Jews (Matthew 15:24), Canaanites (Matthew 15:22), Samaritans (John 4:42), and Gentiles (Matthew 12:18, 21; Luke 2:32; Acts 9:15; 10:45; 11:1, 18). Jesus was "to die for the nation; and not for the nation only, but that He might also gather together into one the children of God who are scattered abroad," that is, around the world (John 11:51–52; 10:16). As a Jew, Peter would have to be convinced in a special way that non-Jews (the world as distinct from Israel) also share in covenantal blessings through the Cross of Christ (Acts 10:1–11:18; 15:1–29; Galatians 2:11–14).

The world as referring to a large group of people (world = general public): "The world has gone after Him" (John 12:19; 7:4; 14:22; 16:21; 18:20). Obviously, the world in this context means a large group of people—not everybody without exception, but everybody without distinction: young and old, male and female, and Jew and Gentile (John 12:20). The Pharisees, who had considerable power over the people, were alarmed that their leadership role would be diluted by this competing religious system.

The world as distinguished from the elect (world = nonelect): "I do not ask on behalf of the world, but of those whom Thou hast given Me; for they are Thine" (John 17:9). Prior to Christ's coming, two worlds existed dividing Jew and Gentile, with some exceptions. Two worlds still exist, but the division is between believers and unbelievers. When we use the word *world* with this meaning in mind, we are referring to those who have not embraced Christ as Lord and Savior.

The world as opposition to the prevailing system of belief that gives meaning and direction to an unbelieving society (world = status quo): "These men who have upset the world [literally, *the inhabited earth*] have come here also" (Acts 17:6). Although a different word is used for *world* (*oikoumene*), the meaning is similar to *kosmos* in application. In the days of the early church, Roman ideology, Roman military strength, and Roman commerce dominated the world. The inhabited earth, as far as the New Testament writers were concerned, was an alien political and religious world (Matthew 24:14; Luke 2:1). The effects of Jesus' redeeming work had an impact on those opposed to the gospel: the world. These gospel opponents understood that allegiance with Jesus would mean that the present king, Caesar, could no longer claim to be lord and god. This is why Jason and his associates were charged with the following: "They all act contrary to the decrees of Caesar, saying that there is another king, Jesus" (Acts 17:7). The use of *world* in this context means the world of pagan Rome dominated by all of its attendant decadence, including its toleration of occult practices (Acts 8:9–11; 13:6–12; 19:19) and worship of rulers (Acts 12:20–24).

The world as a hostile ethical system (world = realm of evil): "Do you not know that friendship with the world is hostility toward God?" (James 4:4). This usage of "world," as well as that of the point above, are definitions that form the meaning for all the others. What world is James talking about? He has in mind the world of unbelief, not the world as a place or sphere of influence in which to work. The use of *kosmos* in this context is "a widespread disposition and power in man-kind for evil in opposition to God."[14] This is not a gnostic understand-ing of *kosmos* as rejecting creation but is typical of the biblical use of

---

"God does not call on us to escape from the world as a place but to avoid worldliness as a system of belief."

---

kosmos to show antithesis to God's moral order (1 Corinthians 11:32; Ephesians 2:2; 1 John 2:15–17).

> The world is in sin and therefore needs to be saved (John 1:20; 3:17; 4:42; 12:47; 16:8). The world is the place of darkness, ethically speak-ing, into which the light (God's holy Son, Jesus Christ) has shone (John 3:19; 8:12; 9:5; 12:46). The world is *spiritually dead* and thus needs life given to it (John 6:33, 51); this clearly demonstrates that "world" cannot be taken in a natural sense, for the world (understood descriptively as the created order) is animated and alive.[15]

Scripture plainly teaches that Christians are to be in the world (geographically) but not of the world (adopting the religions and ethics of those who reject Christ and His law) (John 15:19; 17:14–16, 18; 1 John 2:15). If the world as a place is to be rejected, then God violated His own prohibition by sending His Son into the world and by taking on human flesh. God does not call on us to escape from the world as a place but to avoid worldliness as a system of belief.

Humanism as a Parallel

The biblical use of *kosmos* to denote evil in opposition to God is a description of the world prioritized and absolutized. Humanism similarly prioritizes and absolutizes man. There was a time when humanism did not have the negative connotations now associated with it. "It was during the Renaissance that the word *humanist* was coined. Initially it only defined a concern for humanity, and many early humanists saw no dichotomy between this and their Christian faith."[16] Gradually humanism has come to mean a naturalistic and materialistic worldview in direct opposition to the Christian worldview. This is a far cry from the usual understanding of the word, an appreciation of the humanities and a concern for humanity.

In a similar way, by the time of the New Testament, the word *world* took on various shades of meaning that are not readily found in the Old Testament. *World* in the Old Testament either describes a place of divine activity (Psalm 9:8), inhabitants (Psalm 17:14), or the earth (Psalm 18:15). By the time of the writing of the New Testament, the world was dominated by the Romans, and before that, the Greeks. Thus Christians understood the world to be corrupt and defiled because it manifested Greek and Roman pagan religions and unethical practices. It was this world that was to be rejected, not the world as a place.

If humanity and the humanities are not to be rejected in our rejection of humanism, the world should not be rejected in our rejection of worldliness. The Bible warns

> against worldliness *wherever* it is found [James 1:27], certainly in the church, and [James] is emphasizing here precisely the importance of Christian involvement in *social* issues. Regrettably, we tend to read the Scriptures as though their rejection of a "worldly" life-style entails a recommendation of an "otherworldly" one.
>
> This approach has led many Christians to abandon the "secular" realm to the trends and forces of secularism. Indeed, because of their two-realm theory, to a large degree, Christians have themselves to blame for the rapid secularization of the West. If political, industrial, artistic, and journalistic life, to mention only these areas, are branded as essentially "worldly," "secular," "profane," and part of the "natural domain of creaturely life," then is it surprising that Christians have not more effectively stemmed the tide of humanism in our culture?[17]

God created everything wholly good (Genesis 1:31). Man, through the Fall, became profane, defiled by sin. Redemption restores both man and creation in Christ. Peter failed to understand the gospel's comprehensive cleansing effects. He could not believe the Gentiles were clean until it was revealed to him: "What God has cleansed, no longer consider unholy" (Acts 10:15; Matthew 15:11; Romans 14:14, 20). The

---

"Scripture, and not the two-dimensional worldview of either secularism or pietistic Christianity, is our guide as we deal with the world."

Fall did not nullify God's pronouncement that the created order "was very good" (Genesis 1:31). The New Testament reinforces the goodness of God's creation: "For everything created by God is good, and nothing is to be rejected, if it is received with gratitude; for it is sanctified by means of the word of God and prayer" (1 Timothy 4:4–5).

Scripture, and not the two-dimensional worldview of either secularism or pietistic Christianity, is our guide as we deal with the world. God "became flesh, and dwelt among us" (John 1:14) in this world! We, as Christ's disciples, are to carry out His mission in the world. Jesus worked in His earthly father's shop as a carpenter, affirming the goodness of the created order and the value of physical labor. We can do no less.

2

"INVOLVEMENT IN THE WORLD IS NOT 'SPIRITUAL'"

Recently a historian commented on what he had observed of the Christian faith in America: "Socially irrelevant, even if privately engaging."

OS GUINNESS

In Egypt, in the middle of the third century, an ascetic named Antonius secluded himself from the world after being impressed by the story of the rich young ruler (Mark 10:17–27). He sold all his possessions and distributed the money to the poor. "He then said farewell to the world, to relations and friends, and lived alone—first near his home, then in a tomb, later in a disused fort, and finally on a mountain. Twice a year his friends brought him food, which he ate with a little salt. He drank nothing but water. He decided not to comb or cut his hair, except once a year, at Easter. He never took a bath. . . . Antonius, we are told, lived until he was 106 years of age."[1]

There are other accounts of even more misguided super-spiritual saints. The Stylites or Pillar Saints lived on top of a pillar or *stylos* (the Greek word for *pillar*). Pillar Saints followed the example of an ascetic named Simeon who lived in the fifth century. "Simeon imagined that by living on the top of a pillar his soul would benefit. Beginning with a pillar about six feet high, and gradually increasing its height, he ended up by living for over thirty years on a pillar sixty feet high."[2]

How Much of an Example?

Jesus was supposedly the example for this type of "spirituality" since He did not marry or own property. Other passages may have been used to support the ascetic lifestyle: "The foxes have holes, and the birds of the air have nests; but the Son of Man has nowhere to lay His head" (Matthew 8:20). These escapists seem to have overlooked how Jesus blessed the marriage relationship (John 2:1–11) and never condemned the use of private property, although He did warn of the dangers of riches when they hold a more significant place in the Christian's life than does God Himself (Mark 10:17–31; 1 Timothy 6:10).

Teachers of a false spirituality in the first-century church were forbidding marriage and advocating abstaining from foods, even though "God has created [them] to be gratefully shared in by those who believe and know the truth" (1 Timothy 4:3–4). Decrees such as "Do not handle, do not taste, do not touch!" were set up by some as obligatory for a doctrine of supposed true spirituality. The Apostle Paul clearly stated that they have "the *appearance* of wisdom in self-made religion and self-abasement and severe treatment of the body, but are of *no value* against fleshly indulgence" (Colossians 2:21, 23, emphasis added). In a word, true spirituality is not enhanced by abstaining from the good creation God has created and those institutions He has ordained for the proper government of the world (Romans 13:1–4).

Spirituality is not measured by either a physical or philosophical withdrawal from the world. The Christian who claims he is spiritual because he has distanced himself from the world by not getting involved in the reformation process is a spiritual heir of the "Pillar Saints." Such practices and attitudes are contrary to the words of Jesus when He writes: "Let your light shine before men in such a way that they may see your good works, and glorify your Father who is in heaven" (Matthew 5:16). The Bible surely tells us that we are not of the world (John 17:14), and that we are to "come out from their midst and be separate" (2 Corinthians 6:17), but nowhere are we told to retreat from the world, for Jesus has sent us into the world (John 17:18):

> To be Spiritual is to be guided and motivated by the Holy Spirit. It means obeying His commands as recorded in the Scriptures. The Spiritual man is not someone who floats in midair and hears eerie voices. The Spiritual man is the man who does what the Bible says (Romans 8:4-8). This means, therefore, that we *are* supposed to get involved in life. God wants us to apply Christian standards everywhere, in every area. Spirituality does not mean retreat and withdrawal from life.[3]

Spiritual does not mean "made up of spirit." "Spirit" is not a ghost-like substance that inhabits the truly spiritual Christian. The adjective,

---

"We have been redeemed and rescued from the pollution of the world. This does not mean that we are to turn our backs on life."

---

as in "spiritual man" and "spiritual body," does not mean "ethereal," "incorporeal," "immaterial," or "unworldly" as in *The Ghost and Mrs. Muir* or *The Ghost and Mr. Chicken*.

Spirituality is measured by "good works, which God prepared beforehand, that we should walk in them" (Ephesians 2:10). Good works manifest themselves at the personal level as the Christian exhibits the fruit of the Spirit (Galatians 5:22–24), at the family level as children obey their parents (Ephesians 6:1), at the business level where employers pay a promised wage (Deuteronomy 24:15), at the judicial level where all should be considered equal before the law (Leviticus 24:22), and at the civil level where Caesar is paid his due and God His (Matthew 22:21).

We have been redeemed and rescued from the pollution of the world. This does not mean that we are to turn our backs on life. Rather, we are to avoid all participation in the world's uncleanness. "Christians, indeed, as our Lord taught, are the *light of the world*; this they cannot be if their light is hidden or withdrawn. Thus they are to let their light shine before men (Matthew 5:14ff.), though at the same time shunning the depravities of unregenerate society and of unchristian worship."[4]

Inside-Out Religion

A prevailing and false understanding of true spirituality results when the gospel is turned in on itself. To be spiritual, in the modern and corrupt sense, means to *internalize* the effects of the Holy Spirit's regenerating work on the sinner "dead in . . . trespasses and sins" (Ephesians 2:1). The weakness of this definition is not that spiritual "renewal starts in the private world, but that *it ends there too*."[5] While there is an internal and spiritual reign of Christ in every believer, there must also be an external expression of that internal faith. This is the good Samaritan faith whereby Jesus tells us to "Go and *do* the same" (Luke 10:37, emphasis added); that is, to take responsibility for all who need our care and help. Jesus does reign in the hearts of His saints. This is the necessary first step:

> The internal, spiritual reign of Christ as Savior and Lord must not be overlooked or minimized in importance. One cannot enter into the kingdom of God apart from spiritual rebirth: "Truly, truly I say unto you, except one be born from above, he cannot see the kingdom of God" (John 3:3). Those who are redeemed have already been transferred into the kingdom of God's beloved Son (Colossians 1:13) and as such appreciate that "the kingdom of God is . . . righteousness and peace and joy in the Holy Spirit" (Romans 14:17).[6]

But if the new birth stops with growth on the inside, then it is not true saving faith, just like a light that is hidden under a bushel is not a real light (Matthew 5:14–16). Encouraging someone to "be warmed and be filled" is not an expression of true faith (James 2:16). True spirituality is the Christian faith manifested. Jesus exhibited His love for the world in *deeds* of love and righteousness.

Spiritual Things

As has been pointed out, to be spiritual means to be governed by the Holy Spirit in thoughts, words, and deeds. For many, however, spirituality is confined to the individual exclusive of any external manifestation that would affect the material world. Biblical language alone mitigates against such an interpretation. For example, the devil and his demons are spiritual (nonphysical) and evil:

> And I saw coming out of the mouth of the dragon and out of the mouth of the beast and out of the mouth of the false prophet, three *unclean spirits* like frogs; for they are *spirits of demons*, performing signs, which go out to the kings of the whole world, to gather them together for the war of the great day of God, the Almighty. (Revelation 16:13–14, emphasis added)

There are "deceitful spirits" (1 Timothy 4:1), "unclean spirits" (Revelation 18:2), and spirits of "error" (1 John 4:6). There are even "spiritual forces of wickedness" (Ephesians 6:12).

On the other hand, Jesus has a body, and He is good, without sin (2 Corinthians 5:21). Jesus was raised with His body. Scripture tells us that Jesus shared in "flesh and blood" (Hebrews 2:14). He who denies that Jesus Christ has come in the flesh "is the deceiver and the antichrist" (2 John 7; 1 John 4:1–3).

> [Jesus] is today fleshly, earthly, temporal, although [presently] our eyes behold him not. This is the meaning of the Incarnation. The Docetists,[7] embarrassed with the corporeality of the Gospel, attempted to construct a non-material Saviour; later Gnostics argued that only the spiritual (by which they meant the inward, immortal, eternal) aspects of Christ's nature were of saving efficacy.
>
> The early church stoutly rejected this heresy. They defended the fleshly, earthly, and visible aspects of the Messiah. Man beheld his glory (John 1:14); he was *heard* with human ears and *touched* with human hands (1 John 1:1). To be a genuine Christian it was necessary to confess the Messiah had come in the flesh (1 John 4:2).[8]

If a person is a Christian, then he or she is animated, made alive, by the Holy Spirit. Being spiritual does not mean that he or she is no longer to be concerned with things related to this world, things we might describe as material. Spirit and matter are not opposites in biblical theology. "Since Greek adjectives ending in-*ikos* denote an ethical or dynamic relation, not a material one, *pneumatikos* [spiritual] means 'animated by the spirit' or 'controlled by the spirit.' This 'spirit' refers either to the Holy Spirit or the human spirit as transformed by the divine Spirit."[9] This Holy Spirit (Acts 13:2), a "spirit of truth" (1 John 4:6), "spiritual things" (1 Corinthians 9:11), "spiritual food" (10:3), a "spiritual body" (15:44), "spiritual sacrifices" (1 Peter 2:5), "spiritual wisdom and understanding" (Colossians 1:9), and "ministering spirits, sent out to render service for the sake of those who will inherit salvation" (Hebrews 1:14).

So then, the issue is not spirituality over against non-spirituality. Rather, we must determine whose spirit will be used in determining how we should live in the world: the Spirit of God or the spirit of antichrist? This is why John tells us to "test the spirits" (1 John 4:1). Paul tells us, "Whether, then, you eat or drink or *whatever you do*, do all to the glory of God" (1 Corinthians 10:31, emphasis added).

All areas of life are spiritual, even the realm of politics. "We are so used to thinking of spirituality as withdrawal from the world and human affairs that it is hard to think of it as political. Spirituality is personal and private, we assume, while politics is public. But such a dichotomy drastically diminishes spirituality, construing it as a relationship to God without implications for one's relationship to the surrounding world."[10] Of course, this is what the humanists hope Christians will continue to believe as they pursue the realm of politics with a vengeance. "The notion that we can be related to God and not to the world—that we can practice a spirituality that is not political—is in conflict with the Christian understanding of God."[11] God created the realm of politics in the same way that He created the family and church.

The Sacred/Secular Myth

Related to the issue of true spirituality is the distinction that many Christians make between the realms often described as sacred and secular. The first view (humanism) maintains that all that really matters is the world in which we live and the physical universe that surrounds us.

Only those things that can be evaluated by the senses are real and ultimately important. Any other proposal for meaning beyond the material is myth, legend, or superstition. This view goes by various names: secularism, materialism, and naturalism.

The other view, which is often advanced as the "Christian view," says all that matters are affairs relative to the world to come—things sacred. The world in which we live, because it is seen as our temporary

---

"All areas of life are spiritual, even the realm of politics."

---

home and will one day be judged, should hold little concern for the Christian. There is no hope for the redemption of any part of it. All earthly pursuits are "secular," and thus, outside the scope of Christian living. Therefore, while Christians may involve themselves in "earthly things" out of necessity (e.g., food, clothing, and shelter), they cannot bring with them a distinctly biblical position on any so-called secular subject since God's Word is directed to spiritual things only: the sacred.

Of course, the biblical position finds error in both extremist opinions. The Bible is concerned with this world and the world to come. Heaven is the pattern for our living on the earth. We are to pray that "Thy Kingdom comes" and that "Thy will be done, on earth *as it is in heaven*," and this includes things of this world such as praying for "our daily bread" (Matthew 6:10–11, emphasis added), something we must work for since Paul tells us that the person who does not work does not eat (2 Thessalonians 3:10). We are not told to deny the earth because of the existence of heaven (things spiritual), or to repudiate this age (things secular) because of the glories of the age to come.

It should be pointed out that the word *secular* has not always had the negative connotation given to it by many in the Christian community. For most people in our day, *secular* means nonreligious, and, thus, something less than spiritual. For example, a businessman is involved in secular work while a priest or minister is engaged in spiritual work, usually described as "full-time Christian service." Christians have fallen for the trap set by the secularists who want to keep religion out of anything that is not directly related to church work and the Sunday morning worship hour. The biblical view asserts that all of life is secular; that is, any calling that recognizes God's sovereignty in this age is a holy calling. And all of life is spiritual or religious; that is, each of our callings should be governed by Scripture for God's glory.

> Both [John] Calvin and [Martin] Luther insisted that "secular" vocations were as important as "religious callings" and that it is possible to serve God in any honest and useful job. Calvinism encouraged diligent work and thrifty habits in worldly duties as a way of promoting the general welfare and glorifying God. This "Protestant ethic" was especially endorsed by Puritanism and applied to scientific work. This was reinforced by attitudes of self-restraint, simplicity and diligence. The study of nature was divinely sanctioned since it would reveal God's handiwork and exemplify orderly activity. The Puritans believed science could work for the glory of God and the benefit of society.[12]

Unfortunately, many Christians no longer believe that all of life is religious. They believe that to be involved in "secular work," that is, work that has meaning for the here and now, is something less than spiritual. This is a myth.

The Religion of Secularism

Having asserted the spiritual nature of all reality, we still need to consider a secular worldview that seeks to absolutize the things of this world. A different spirit energizes man without God. This is the religion of humanism called secularism. It is the secular, this age, made absolute and final. There is no God, no heaven, no spirit other than the spirit that resides in man. Man is his own god, and this world is all there is. Whereas Christianity was considered to be the solution to man's problems, now the religion of secularism has taken its place. Secularism is essentially messianic. It offers a plan of salvation for a lost planet:

> Humanism has become the most messianic of the idolatrous religions of the West. Anthropologist Margaret Mead included in her autobiography

a frank acknowledgement that it was a religious belief and called urgently for its spread throughout the world. This is why Milton Friedman described [John Kenneth] Galbraith as "a missionary seeking converts." The same urge was behind Erich Fromm's *tour de force*, the transformation of the Old Testament into a defense of radical humanism.[13]

Keeping the dangers of getting involved in this world in mind, let us remember that salvation comes only through the regenerating work of God's Holy Spirit. Nothing in this world can save us. There can be

---

"If the Christian is not involved in the transformation process with the Christian view of spirituality, then be assured that the humanists will be ready with their version."

---

no neutrality here. If the Christian is not involved in the transformation process with the Christian view of spirituality, then be assured that the humanists will be ready with their version. The rise of New Age humanism is one indication that the faltering West is looking for a new spirit to breathe life into the decaying corpse of humanism.

"THE BIBLE IS ONLY CONCERNED ABOUT SALVATION"

"The Gospel . . . is not confined to a repentance and faith that have no connection with social or civil duties. The Evangel of Christ is an all-embracing theme. It is the vital force in earth and in heaven. . . . The Cross is the centre of the spiritual, and therefore of the material universe." The divine touchstone before which "literature, science, politics, business, the status of society, all charities, all reforms" must be brought to test.

GILBERT HAVEN

A New York judge used the Bible to determine the amount of bail to be paid by a former Episcopal church treasurer accused of embezzling $267,000 from his congregation. Judge Robert Meehan set bail at $534,000, "pointing out that the sum was $2.00 for every $1.00 he allegedly stole. The judge said he chose the bail figure because 'it has a religious message, that if you steal you have to pay back two-fold' [Exodus 22:4, 7]."[1] Charles Colson, president of Prison Fellowship, has been

calling for the contemporary application of the Bible as the solution to
prison reform:

> Recently I addressed the Texas legislature. . . . I told them that the
> only answer to the crime problem is to take nonviolent criminals out
> of our prisons and make them pay back their victims with restitution.
> This is how we can solve the prison crowding problem.
>
> The amazing thing was that afterwards they came up to me one
> after another and said things like, "That's a tremendous idea. Why
> hasn't anyone thought of that?" I had the privilege of saying to them,
> "Read Exodus 22. It is only what God said to Moses on Mount Sinai
> thousands of years ago."[2]

As these examples demonstrate, there is more to the Bible than its
message of eternal salvation, although this is its primary theme. God
has laid down specific guidelines on how men should operate in a world
infected by sin.

New Heart, New Life

Regeneration is the starting point for the development of any social
theory. Little can change for good in the broader culture unless man
changes. The only way man can change is through the regenerating
work of the Holy Spirit. Those dead in "trespasses and sins" (Ephesians
2:1) must have a new heart and a new spirit. The heart of stone must
be removed and a heart of flesh substituted. This is God's work. God's
Spirit must be in us before we can walk in His statutes. The result will
be that we "will be careful to observe [His] ordinances" (Ezekiel 36:26–
27). The New Testament summarizes it this way: "If any man is in
Christ, he is a new creature; the old things passed away; behold, new
things have come" (2 Corinthians 5:17). All of this requires a belief in
the sovereignty of God. Only God can make dead men live (John
11:25–26). Only God can make a dead culture thrive. Noted scholar
and author Rousas J. Rushdoony summarizes it this way:

> The key to remedying the [modern] situation is *not* revolution, nor
> any kind of resistance that works to subvert law and order. The New
> Testament abounds in warnings against disobedience and in summons

to peace. *The key is regeneration, propagation of the gospel, and the conversion of men and nations to God's law-word. . . .*
    Clearly, there is no hope for man except in regeneration.[3]

Politics, a conservative economic policy, and other social agendas are not the ultimate answers to man's dilemma. Man is a sinner in need

---

"Regeneration is the starting point for the development of any social theory. Little can change for good in the broader culture unless man changes."

---

of salvation. He cannot make proper evaluations of how he ought to live in the world until he has a new heart that guides a new mind.

The Domino Effect of Reform

A direct relationship between personal salvation and reform can be found in a number of places in Scripture. Zacchaeus not only found Jesus, he also found a new lifestyle. He restored what he had unlawfully taken from others (Luke 19:8; Exodus 22:1; Leviticus 6:5; Numbers 5:7; 2 Samuel 12:6). His personal regeneration had societal and civil impact. Keep in mind that Zacchaeus used his office as a tax gatherer backed up by the power of the Roman civil government to line his pockets at the expense of the citizenry (Luke 19:2). Consider what it would mean for our nation if politicians who claim the name of Christ applied biblical principles to their work. Jesus' public ministry was the perfect mixture of evangelism and worldly concern. He went about teaching and preaching (Matthew 4:23; 9:35) and doing good and healing (Acts 10:38).
    In a similar vein, "John the Baptist told tax-gatherers and soldiers not to use their positions to extort money (Luke 3:12-14). When Paul had the opportunity to speak with Felix he talked about 'righteousness,

self-control and the judgment to come' (Acts 24:25). James warned the rich of the judgment that must come to those who had defrauded a workman of his wages (James 5:1–6)."[4]

The first efforts of the early church were to minister to the worldly needs of its members. The gospel included works of mercy, works that had an impact on seemingly mundane issues like seeing that widows were not "being overlooked in the daily serving of food" (Acts 6:1). In our modern welfare-state economy, those least able to care for themselves are most often turned over to government agencies for assistance. Supposedly these are secular activities that are solely the province of civil government. This view, however, was not the view of the early church (1 Timothy 5:3). James writes that "pure and undefiled religion" consists of visiting "orphans and widows in their distress" (James 1:27). In the same verse he exhorts Christians to keep themselves "unstained by the world." Therefore, it cannot be considered "worldly" to involve oneself in activities that are not directly related to proclamation of the gospel.

The Apostle Paul makes similar application when he writes: "Let him who steals steal no longer; but rather let him labor, performing with his own hands what is good, in order that he may have something to share with him who has need" (Ephesians 4:28). In another place, Paul exhorts Christians to forsake the unrighteous civil courts and establish their own courts for settling disputes among the brethren (1 Corinthians 6:1–11).

Reconciling the World

God created the world good (Genesis 1:31), and even after the entrance of sin into the world, "everything created by God is [still] good, and nothing is to be rejected, if it is received with gratitude; for it is sanctified by means of the word of God and prayer" (1 Timothy 4:4–5). "Because the physical world is revealed as good it is worthy of detailed and devoted study. Because it is real such efforts will not be irrelevant or illusory. However, the goodness of creation does not imply a realm of perfection."[5]

The world is good and the object of God's redeeming work: "God was in Christ reconciling the *world* to Himself" (2 Corinthians 5:19, emphasis added). God's purpose is to redeem man in all his undertakings. Nothing is left outside of God's redemptive scope. "As Abraham Kuyper said, there is not one inch of creation of which Christ doesn't

---

"God's purpose is to redeem man in all his undertakings. Nothing is left outside of God's redemptive scope."

---

say 'Mine.'"[6] In addition, God's Word "is inspired . . . and profitable for teaching, for reproof, for correction, for training in righteousness; that the man of God may be adequate, equipped for every good work" (2 Timothy 3:16–17). After further study, we learn that the Bible has some very specific things to say about how God's good creation ought to work and how man ought to run it under His lordship and direction.

The following list of topics demonstrates that the Bible is more than a book on how we can get to heaven (although it is that); it is also designed to give us a pattern for how we should be living in the world over which God has made His image-bearers His stewards. The Lord taught Christians to pray, "Thy kingdom come. *Thy will be done, on earth as it is in heaven*" (Matthew 6:10, emphasis added). How do we know God's will for this earth? The Bible tells us. The following table shows some of the issues the Bible addresses.

Family Issues

- Parental authority (Ephesians 6:1–4)
- Inheritance (Proverbs 13:22)
- Discipline (Proverbs 13:24)
- Marriage (Genesis 1:27–28; Matthew 19:3–12; 1 Corinthians 7:2)
- Education (Proverbs 22:6)
- Charity (1 Timothy 5:8)

- Care for the aged (1 Timothy 5:3–13)
- Leadership (1 Timothy 3:1–7)

Economic Issues[7]

- Debt (Proverbs 3:27–28; Romans 13:8)
- Borrowing (Exodus 22:25; Psalm 37:21; Proverbs 22:7; Isaiah 24:2)
- Lending (Exodus 22:25; Deuteronomy 15:6; Psalm 37:26)
- Interest (Deuteronomy 23:19–20; Proverbs 22:26–27)
- Inflation (Proverbs 25:4–5; Isaiah 1:22–26; Ezekiel 22:18–22)
- Helping the needy (Leviticus 25:35–37; Deuteronomy 15:7-11; 24:14–15)
- Inheritance (Psalm 17:13–15; Proverbs 13:22; 19:14; 20:21)
- Work (Genesis 2:15; 3:19; Exodus 20:8–11; Proverbs 10:5; Ecclesiastes 3:13; Acts 16:14; Ephesians 4:28; 2 Thessalonians 3:10–12)
- Wages (Deuteronomy 24:14–15; Jeremiah 22:13; Luke 10:7; 1 Corinthians 9:7–12; 1 Timothy 5:18)
- Employee/employer relations (Leviticus 25:53; Proverbs 6:6–9; 10:4; 27:18; 28:19)
- Savings (Proverbs 6:6–8; 21:20; 28:20; 1 Timothy 6:9)
- Fraud (Ephesians 4:28; 1 Thessalonians 4:6)
- Investments (Psalm 112:5)

Civil Issues[8]

- Civil authority (Matthew 22:15–22; Romans 13:1–4; 1 Peter 2:13–17)
- Citizenship (Leviticus 24:22; Numbers 15:22–31; Acts 22:22–29)
- Bribery (Exodus 23:8; Deuteronomy 10:17; 16:19–20)
- Taxation (1 Samuel 8; Proverbs 27:18; Matthew 22:17–21; Luke 3:12–13)
- The military (Numbers 1:2–3; 26:2; 31:3–7; Deuteronomy 20:5–8)
- National defense (2 Chronicles 26:6–15)
- Civil loyalties (Acts 5:29)

Legal Issues

- The judicial system (Exodus 18; 1 Corinthians 6:1–11)
- Laws regarding perverting and obstructing justice (Exodus 23:1–2, 6; Leviticus 19:15; Deuteronomy 16:19–20)
- Perjury (Exodus 20:16; Leviticus 19:12; Deuteronomy 19:16–20)
- Murder (Exodus 20:13; 21:12)
- Assault (Exodus 21:18–27; Leviticus 24:19–20)
- Kidnapping (Exodus 21:16; Deuteronomy 24:7)
- Slander (Leviticus 19:16)
- Stealing (Exodus 20:15; 22:1–12)
- Arson (Exodus 22:6)
- Property violations (Deuteronomy 19:14)
- Damages (Leviticus 6:1–5; 24:19–20; Exodus 22:4–6)
- Restitution (Exodus 21:18–19, 22–25, 28–30, 32; 22:1–9; Luke 19:8; Ephesians 4:28)

Ethical Issues

- Abortion (Exodus 21:22–25)
- Homosexuality (Leviticus 18:22; 20:13)
- Rape (Deuteronomy 22:25–29)
- Prostitution (Deuteronomy 23:17)
- Incest (Leviticus 18:6–18; Deuteronomy 22:30)
- Adultery (Exodus 20:14; Leviticus 20:10; Deuteronomy 5:18; 22:22–25)
- Bestiality (Exodus 22:19; Leviticus 18:23)

In addition, there are biblical principles related to sanitation (Deuteronomy 23:13), education (Deuteronomy 6:4–9), environmental issues (Deuteronomy 20:19–20), building safety (Deuteronomy 22:8), and many other issues.[9] If Christians refuse to leaven these areas with the life-transforming work of the gospel, then the world will be leavened with the "leaven of the Pharisees and the leaven of Herod" (Mark 8:15). When the Word of God is rejected as the standard for godly living in this world, a substitute standard fills the vacuum. The leaven of the Pharisees substitutes the law of God with man-made traditions: Jesus "was also saying to them, 'You nicely set aside the commandment of God in order to keep your tradition'" (Mark 7:9). The leaven of Herod places the state over the will of God: "These men who have upset the world have come here also; . . . they all act contrary to the decrees of Caesar, saying that there is another king, Jesus" (Acts 17:6–7).

Government at all levels is only as good as the people who create it. Family, church, and civil governments reflect how individuals think and act, whether good or bad. At the civil level, a nation gets what it votes for. Civil government, no matter how righteously conceived, cannot make people better. Leadership, like water, rises to its own level, the righteousness of the people. In short, good government depends on good people, and we get good people through the preaching of the gospel. We get good deeds from good people who are willing to apply God's "Good Book" to every area of life. We are commanded to show our good works so those without Christ can glorify our God who is in heaven (Matthew 5:16). If our religion remains a private affair, then it is good for nothing, only to be trampled underfoot by unbelievers (v. 13).

PART 2

THE CHRISTIAN
AND MORALITY

"YOU CANNOT LEGISLATE MORALITY"

What Moses brought down from Mt. Sinai were not the Ten Suggestions. They are commandments. Are, not were. The sheer brilliance of the Ten Commandments is that they codify in a handful of words acceptable human behavior, not just for then or now, but for all time. Language evolves. Power shifts from one nation to another. Messages are transmitted with the speed of light. Man erases one frontier after another. And yet we and our behavior and the command- ments governing that behavior remain the same.

TED KOPPEL

L adies and Gentlemen, young and old. This may seem an unusual procedure, speaking to you before the picture begins, but we have an unusual subject: the birth of freedom. The story of Moses." Yes, it was an unusual way to begin a movie. These are the introductory words of Cecil B. de Mille, the director of *The Ten Commandments* (1956), starring Charlton Heston and Yul Brynner. But de Mille had something more in mind than just the making of a movie. He considered the topic of his movie to be so important that he came out on stage to deliver a short but powerful statement on the nature of freedom under the law of God:

> The theme of this picture is whether men ought to be ruled by God's laws or whether they are to be ruled by the whims of a dictator like Rameses. Are men the property of the State or are they free souls under God? This same battle continues throughout the world today.

All law is a reflection of some moral code. It is impossible to avoid imposing morality on people or legislating morality. Laws against theft and murder are legislated, and they reflect a moral code. There are few people who would object to laws being made that would punish thieves and murderers. And yet, such laws impose a moral system on all of us. Although thieves and murderers might object, no one is calling for these laws to be rescinded because they impose a moral code.

Then there are the questions that arise defining what it means to steal and murder. At one time, the general consensus held that abortion was murder. Now the moral climate has shifted. Abortion has been legalized. What once constituted murder, now is considered a cherished right that should be protected by law. Pro-abortion advocates believe it is *immoral* to deny a woman the right to an abortion. They work to impose laws on the whole society to protect the "moral rights" of those who want abortions:

> Every system of government exists to produce or enforce certain laws, and every law necessarily entails a set of moral assumptions. All morality—even that which is usually supposed to be, or touted as being, based upon an "irreligious" or "anti-religious" philosophical foundation—is ultimately religious in its nature, since it is founded upon a set of pretheoretical presuppositions, fundamental assumptions about the nature of reality, about God, man, and things, which are taken on (a usually unacknowledged) faith. In this deepest sense, then, the question for every legal system is not whether it will be based upon "religion" but rather which religion or religious philosophy will be its foundation?[1]

One system of morality is set against another in the debate over legislation. Moral persuasion is almost always used. "It is immoral to have people living in cardboard boxes or in abandoned automobiles when there is so much wealth in a country like the United States," advocates for the homeless remark. Champions of peace push their cause with, "It's immoral to make bombs when there are so many needy

---

"All law is a reflection of some moral code. It is impossible to avoid imposing morality on people or legislating morality."

---

people in the world." They work for change at the state and federal levels to get backing for their cause using moral persuasion.

Whose Morality?

"In a scene from the recent Western, *Silverado*, set before law and order reached the frontier, an old black homesteader is murdered by ruthless cattle ranchers. When the old man's son discovers the body he says sorrowfully, 'This ain't right.'"[2] But why "ain't" it right? The question, then, is not "will morality be legislated?" but "whose morality will be legislated?" Ted Turner, self-professed humanist and "News King," did not deny that there needs to be a moral code when he came up with his own set of "ten commandments." He concluded that there needs to be a *new* moral code based on *his* view of morality. Turner said:

> We're living with outmoded rules. The rules we're living under is [*sic*] the Ten Commandments, and I bet nobody here even pays much attention to 'em, because they are too old. When Moses went up on the mountain, there were no nuclear weapons, there was no poverty. Today, the commandments wouldn't go over. Nobody around likes to be commanded.

Has Turner read the Ten Commandments lately? Does he really want us to believe that laws against theft and murder are "outmoded rules"? I wonder how he would respond if some of his employees began to steal from him? If people don't like to be commanded under the "outmoded rules" called the Ten Commandments, then why should they want to be commanded under Turner's commandments? Who will enforce Turner's new commandments? What will the punishment be for not complying?

We can't live without rules and a moral code. Even humanists like Turner acknowledge this. Besides, there was poverty in Moses' day, and the law that came from God to Moses on Mount Sinai set forth detailed solutions to handle poverty.

Judgment is not based on the wishes of the few or the pressures of the mighty. Judgment can only be secured when we turn to a law that rests outside the partisan interests of fallen men. Judgment must rest on objective norms of law and justice. Should we appeal to the latest polling statistics? Is the Supreme Court the final appeal? Whose law is right? Why should we listen to Ted Turner and not Adolf Hitler?

Autonomy as Law

What people often object to is the legislation of morality that affects them personally. Some women want abortion to be legal so they can choose the procedure if a birth control device fails. They object to any legislation that would make abortion illegal. But these same abortion proponents would not want legislation that allowed husbands to beat their wives. They would want anti-wife-beating legislation imposed on their husbands. In short, law or morality is perceived as personal autonomy (self-law): "I can do whatever I want to do." But clearly this results in anarchy. Again, there is no escape from legislating morality.

> The statement, "You can't legislate morality," is a dangerous half-truth and even a lie, because *all* legislation is concerned with morality. Every law on the statute books of every civil government is either an example of enacted morality or it is procedural thereto. Our laws are all moral laws, representing a system of morality. Laws against manslaughter and murder are moral laws; they echo the commandment "Thou shalt not kill." Laws against theft are commandments against stealing. Slander and libel laws, perjury laws, enact the moral requirement "Thou shalt not bear false witness." Traffic laws are moral laws

also: their purpose is to protect life and property; again, they reflect the Ten Commandments. Laws concerning police and court procedures have a moral purpose also, to further justice and to protect law and order. Every law on the statute books is concerned with morality or with the procedures for the enforcement of law, and all law is concerned with morality. We may disagree with the morality of a law, but we cannot deny the moral concern of law. Law is concerned with right and wrong; it punishes and restrains evil and protects the good, and this is exactly what morality is about. It is impossible to have law without morality behind the law, because all law is simply enacted morality.[3]

The Bible and Morality

Consider the Bible. God's standard of justice is the same for all His creatures, whether Jew or Gentile, believer or unbeliever. This even includes nations which consider themselves to be non-Christian. Some believe that because they do not acknowledge God as Lord and King that they are exempt from following the law of God. In this case, they object to any law that has a religious origin. But laws against murder and theft are deeply rooted in religious traditions, specifically Christian tradition. The Ten Commandments are noted for their prohibitions against numerous crimes that are a part of our present legal system.

Under the Old Covenant

Sodom and Gomorrah enjoyed no such exemption from the laws of the Bible: "Now the men of Sodom were wicked exceedingly and sinners *against the* LORD" (Genesis 13:13, emphasis added). This corrupt city was destroyed for breaking God's law, in particular, the sin of homosexuality (Genesis 19:4–5; Leviticus 18:22; 20:13).[4] Jonah went to preach to the non-Israelite city of Nineveh because of its national sins. If the Ninevites were not obligated to keep the law of God—a law supported by religion—then how could they be expected to repent, and why was God about to judge them? (Jonah 3).

The stranger, an individual *outside* the covenant community of Israel, was obligated to obey the law of God: "There shall be one standard for you; it shall be for the stranger as well as the native, for I am the LORD your God" (Leviticus 24:22; Numbers 15:16; Deuteronomy 1:16–17). God's law was being imposed upon them. Failure to comply meant judgment, both temporal and eternal.

The Law as given to Israel was also a standard for the nations surrounding Israel. When these nations heard of the righteous judgments within Israel, they would remark with wonder: "Surely this great nation is a wise and understanding people" (Deuteronomy 4:6). The psalmist proclaims to the kings and judges of the earth to "take warning . . . [and] worship the LORD with reverence . . ." and to "do homage to the Son" (Psalm 2:10–12):

> It is striking how frequently the other nations are called upon in the Psalms to recognize and to honor God, and how complete is the witness of the prophets against the nations surrounding Israel. God does not exempt other nations from the claim of his righteousness; he requires their obedience and holds them responsible for their apostasy and degeneration [e.g., Amos 1:3–2:5].[5]

Isn't this the imposition of God's morality on the world?

Under the New Covenant

The New Testament presupposes the validity of the imposition of God's moral code on the world. John the Baptist used the law of God to confront Herod—an Idumean—in his adulterous affair: "Herod . . . had John arrested and bound in prison on account of Herodias, the wife of his brother Philip, because he had married her. For John had been saying to Herod, 'It is not lawful for you to have your brother's wife'" (Mark 6:17–18, emphasis added; Leviticus 20:10; Deuteronomy 22:22). This was more than advice.

The psalmist declares that he will speak of God's "testimonies before kings, and shall not be ashamed" (Psalm 119:46). These testimonies are the commandments which he loves (v. 47). Similarly, Jesus tells His disciples that persecution will give them an opportunity to speak "before governors and kings . . . as a testimony to them and to the Gentiles" (Matthew 10:18).

Notice what John the Baptist told some civil servants who approached him regarding their obligations to the law of God: "Some tax-gatherers also came to be baptized, and they said to him, 'Teacher, what shall we do?' And he said to them, 'Collect no more than what you

---

"There is no area of life where man is exempt from the demands of the law of God."

---

have been ordered to.' And some soldiers were questioning him, saying, 'And what about us, what shall we do?' And he said to them, 'Do not take money from anyone by force, or accuse anyone falsely, and be content with your wages'" (Luke 3:12–14). John referred them to the sixth, ninth, and tenth commandments of the Decalogue (Exodus 20).

Christians are obligated to inform those who rule in the civil sphere of the demands of the law and the consequences of disobedience. There is no area of life where man is exempt from the demands of the law of God. In Romans 13 the civil magistrate is said to be a minister of God who has the responsibility and authority to punish evildoers. As God's servants they are obligated to rule God's way and to impose His law in those areas where the Bible gives the magistrate jurisdiction. Just as a minister in the church is obligated to implement the law of God as it touches on ecclesiastical matters, a civil servant must implement the law of God as it relates to civil affairs. The determination of good and evil must derive from some objective standard. If the magistrate does not impose God's law, then he will impose his own law or the law of those who have the greatest influence.

Paul ends the section dealing with the civil magistrate by quoting from the Ten Commandments and proceeds to tell us that they are summed up in the single commandment "You shall love your neighbor as yourself" (Romans 13:9). But this isn't something unique to the New Testament. Paul quotes from Leviticus 19:18 for this summary of the law. Now, some might want to maintain that a summary ethic of love *supplants* and *replaces* the law. But a summary does not nullify what it summarizes. Does a summary at the end of a chapter in a book nullify and supplant what it summarizes? Of course not. In the same way, love as the summary of the law does not nullify the details of what it summarizes.

Others might want to maintain that love is our sole guide when it comes to ethical behavior since Paul says that he who loves his neighbor has fulfilled the law (Romans 13:10). But the question remains: How do you know when you are loving your neighbor? Again, love without specifics becomes license. Love must always be defined in some way. The law gives definition to love. Besides, did not Paul confirm the law (3:31) which was holy, just, and good? (7:12, 14).

The redemptive work of Jesus does not free us from an obligation to keep the moral law—including the social laws—laid down in the Bible. Scripture shows no instance of an individual, Christian or pagan, who is no longer required to keep the laws outlined in Scripture. Christians are freed from the "curse of the Law" (Galatians 3:13), but not from the demands of the law: "Do we then nullify the Law through faith? May it never be! On the contrary, we establish the Law" (Romans 3:31).

What Cannot Be Legislated

Of course, there is no way that laws can be imposed to make people good. In this sense, it's true that morality should not be imposed or legislated. But making people good is not the function of law. Law, in the biblical sense, is designed to restrain people from doing evil, protect life and property, and set limits for punishment when a violation occurs. But to say that law cannot be legislated in any sense is nonsense.

The law, even with the best intentions in mind, cannot turn devils into angels. If, however, punishment follows the breaking of the law, another individual, seeing that there is punishment (either multiple restitution or death) might be deterred from attempting the same criminal act.

The phrase "you can't legislate morality" has undergone a strange evolution in meaning. Originally the expression meant a person's behavior cannot automatically be altered by simply passing laws; legislation doesn't stop people from doing what they are determined to do. The contemporary meaning of the phrase is that it is wrong or illegitimate to enact legislation that restricts moral behavior.

This is a ridiculous notion.[6]

One final point should be made. There are numerous prohibitions in Scripture, but many of them do not have ecclesiastical or civil punishments attached to them. Sins of the heart are not crimes. Coveting, for example, is a sin, but it is not a crime. If covetousness leads to thievery, then punitive action can be taken only after a theft has occurred. In addition, some acts of disobedience are best handled by the church and her courts (Matthew 18:15–20; 1 Corinthians 6:1–11). Families are also governments that have jurisdictional authority to handle family disputes. All in all, no one can escape the imposition of some moral code.[7]

5

"CHRISTIANS SHOULD REMAIN NEUTRAL"

There is not a square inch of ground in
heaven or on earth or under the earth in
which there is peace between Christ and
Satan. . . . No one can stand back, refus-
ing to become involved. He is involved from
the day of his birth and even from before his
birth. Jesus said: "He that is not with me is
against me, and he that gathered not with
me scattereth abroad." If you say that you
are "not involved" you are in fact involved
in Satan's side.

CORNELIUS VAN TIL

On August 8, 1990, the American Bar Association (ABA) reversed itself on the abortion issue, rescinding "the prochoice stance on abortion it had adopted only six months earlier by a 238 to 106 vote. Prior to the House of Delegates' consideration of the issue last month, the association's general membership voted 885 to 837 in favor of a position of neutrality."[1] What if the ABA had been around when slavery was an issue in this nation? Would a position of neutrality have been acceptable to the slaves? How do you think the proslavery states would have read the stance of neutrality? It would have been business, that is, slavery, as usual. What if the ABA had been operating during Hitler's "final solution" to rid the world of Jews? Are we to believe that neutrality would have been an acceptable position?

An Impossible Position

How can anyone be neutral about anything? God always requires us to make a decision. You are either for Christ or against Him (Matthew 12:30). A decision has to be made. Joshua put it like this to his fellow Israelites: Either serve Jehovah or serve the gods of your fathers. There is nothing in between. To "forsake the LORD" is "to serve other gods" (Joshua 24:16). It's either God or Baal, Christ or Satan.

Elijah asks it this way, "How long will you hesitate between two opinions? If the LORD is God, follow Him; but if Baal, follow him" (1 Kings 18:21). What if the people had decided that they would serve neither Jehovah nor Baal? Their supposed claim of neutrality would have been a decision *against* Jehovah. On Judgment Day, those who have not turned to Christ will not be able to maintain their innocence by claiming that they did not speak against Christ. Neutrality is not an option.

Even One Who Hates You

If a passerby refuses to help an accident victim who is bleeding profusely, he cannot claim neutrality. Even if he decides neither to walk away nor to make an effort to help, he is not being neutral. Standing at the scene and watching a person die is not neutrality. The bystander's inaction has worked to do harm to the accident victim.

The Bible is not silent on the issue of neutrality. Consider what Scripture says about an individual's responsibility in the care of a neighbor's animal:

> You shall not see your countryman's ox or his sheep straying away, and pay no attention to them; you shall certainly bring them back to your countryman. . . . You shall not see your countryman's donkey or his ox

fallen down on the way, and pay no attention to them; you shall certainly help him to raise them up. (Deuteronomy 22:1, 4)

The passage stipulates that "*anything* lost by your countryman" is to be returned (v. 3, emphasis added). Elsewhere in the Bible the stipulation goes still further: "If you meet your *enemy's* ox or his donkey wan-

---

"If a passerby refuses to help an accident victim who is bleeding profusely, he cannot claim neutrality."

---

dering away, you shall surely return it to him. If you see the donkey of one who *hates you* lying helpless under its load, you shall refrain from leaving it to him, you shall surely release it with him" (Exodus 23:4–5, emphasis added). Now, what's true for the *animals* of our neighbors certainly holds true for our *neighbors* who are created in the image of God. There is no possibility of neutrality even in dealings with our enemies!

Silence Would Not Have Been Golden

What if Mordecai and Esther had tried to remain neutral when they learned of Haman's plot to destroy her Jewish countrymen? Silence, neutrality, was not an option, a point that Mordecai was quick to make:

> Do not imagine that you in the king's palace can escape any more than all the Jews. For if you remain silent at this time, relief and deliverance will arise from the Jews from another place and you and your father's house will perish. And who knows whether you have not attained royalty for such a time as this? (Esther 4:13–14)

Esther could have remained silent, and it may have happened that she and her family would have escaped Haman's scheme. But it was only a matter of time before he would have come after her. Her status as royalty would not have saved her for long. She risked death by approaching the king about the plot only because she realized that silence was not neutrality; it was a decision to forsake her people and eventually to forsake God and His Word.

Esther made a direct plea to the king (7:1–6) over against his initial agreement to Haman's plan (3:10–15), a law that, technically, could "not be repealed" (1:19; 8:8). As a result, the king had Haman hanged in the place of Mordecai, Haman's intended victim. The law calling for the extermination of the Jews was repealed (8:3–14). Esther received "the house of Haman" (8:1) and Mordecai was promoted (8:2, 15).

What would have happened if Esther and Mordecai had chosen the path of supposed neutrality? The Jewish people would have suffered greatly, although God would have raised up another savior who would not have remained silent. Relief and deliverance would have arisen for the Jews from another place. Neutrality is never an option with God.

The Samaritan Factor

The New Testament nowhere accepts neutrality as a Christian response to man and his world. A fellow-Jew, beaten, robbed, and left for dead, is ignored by a priest and a Levite. These religious men, to protect themselves from ceremonial uncleanness, "passed by on the other side" (Luke 10:32). Isn't this similar to today's claim of neutrality in the social and political realms by many Christians who want to protect their "spirituality"? To be involved in such secular issues like voting against men and women who support abortion and homosexuality—two grievous sins that destroy unborn human beings and disrupt and ravage the God-ordained family—would mean spiritual defilement. To work for a political candidate would mean less time spent on witnessing, Bible study, prayer, and church services. In addition, don't we often hear that "politics is dirty," inferring that a Christian's "spirituality" will be polluted by such work?

Some might want to assert that while *personal* social activism is permitted, *political* social activism is neither mandated, encouraged, nor approved by Scripture. Christians are to remain politically neutral. But, in fact, the Bible mandates, approves, and encourages both social and political activism. Consider the implications of remaining neutral when it comes to social and political issues. Our failure to involve ourselves

---

"The Bible mandates, approves, and encourages both social and political activism."

---

means that we neglect Jesus' instruction to the lawyer who asked Jesus about the identity of his neighbor:

> "Which of these three do you think proved to be a neighbor to the man who fell into the robbers' hands?" And he said, "The one who showed mercy toward him." And Jesus said to him, "Go and do the same" (Luke 10:36–37).

Political decisions, unlike the single decision of the priest, Levite, and Samaritan, affect millions of citizens. The pregnant woman is our neighbor. The unborn child is our neighbor. Over one million unborn babies are killed each year in the United States. To choose neutrality and base it on the teaching of the Bible is to go against the go-and-do-likewise ethic given to the lawyer who asked about the identity of his neighbor.

Remaining silent over the sodomy issue is equally unbiblical. The young boy who is seduced by a homosexual will most often be enticed by those who have embraced the homosexual deathstyle. Is it neutrality when we allow the legalization of a form of sexual perversion (sodomy), a practice that the Bible says deserves the death penalty? (Leviticus 20:13).

All social and political issues deserve a biblical response by Christians. This will mean studying the newspapers, magazines, and news reports in the light of the Bible. Our political representatives should be scrutinized in terms of what the Bible says about issues relating to civil government.

The Humanist Variety of Neutrality

The perpetuation of the neutrality myth has been used by secular humanists to keep Christians out of the arena where social policy is affected, allowing Christians only a privatized religion. Christians who assert that neutrality is the biblical way have much in common with the humanists at this point. Christians are told, "You can be involved in social issues, but you cannot bring in your religious convictions. You must be neutral." The assumption is that those who are formulating public policy issues are also being neutral. But they are not. Everybody looks at the world in non-neutral terms. Some worldview—some set of presuppositions—is used to evaluate every fact and idea that comes our way. Social policy and everything else we do are determined by these presuppositions. Everybody evaluates life from a certain religious point of view, in terms of what he or she considers to be ultimate authority (e.g., God, man, experience, pragmatism, reason, the will of the people). Even the atheist is not neutral. His public policy statements will be based on the presupposition that there is no God. In fact, denying God's Word a place in public policy discussions because it assumes a religious presupposition is an action against God and His Word.

Here is how one editorial writer describes the way neutrality should operate: Christians can "rant and rave against humanism and feminism and any other 'ism' on Sunday, come Monday, the children belong in school."[2] According to this brand of neutrality, children, parents, and ministers should refrain from expressing their religious convictions, say, in a public school classroom. On Sunday children get religious instruction that should go no further than the four walls of the church and have no greater purpose than personal piety. On Monday through Friday, we are led to believe that children are to receive value-free (i.e., neutral) learning—an impossible task.

The attempts to provide a value-free, supposedly neutral, way of dealing with social issues demonstrate that we have raised a throng of moral illiterates. In our attempts to be neutral regarding morality, we have pushed a generation of young people into the arms of immorality:

When confronted with questions of right and wrong, many more youngsters are guided by what gets them ahead or what makes them feel good than by what their parents or religious authorities say, according to an ongoing study of moral development.[3]

This is the fruit of the humanist insistence that when it comes to morality, parents, teachers, and ministers should remain neutral. Children are to make up their own minds when it comes to moral questions.

"The attempts to provide a value-free, supposedly neutral, way of dealing with social issues demonstrate that we have raised a throng of moral illiterates."

They have. "Overall, 21 percent of elementary-school youngsters told researchers they would try to copy answers or glance at another student's test."[4] The percentages do not get any better as the children get older. "Sixty-five percent of high school students said they would cheat on a test if they didn't know the answers."[5] The conclusion of the study? "There is no one underlying set of assumptions that guides the moral life of American children."[6] We should not be surprised, since moral education has been rejected in favor of moral neutrality. Moral neutrality has brought about "moral illiteracy," which has produced immorality.

A Double Standard

While Christians line up behind the neutrality doctrine, the humanists are establishing their agenda in violation of their own rhetoric. How can they get away with it? A more basic question should be, why do we let them get away with it? So then, Christians dutifully believe the secularist's version of neutrality, believing that it is a biblical and constitutional principle, and then wonder why every competing worldview finds its way into the classroom except biblical Christianity. Chuck Colson describes the outlandish but predictable results:

> A friend I greatly respect was speaking, citing one example after another. They were bizarre stories: like the high-school students informed that they could not wear their Fellowship of Christian Athletes T-shirts to school (though satanic T-shirts were okay); or the court decision forcing Zion, Illinois, to change its 88-year-old city seal because it included religious symbols. Or the fact that *The Last Temptation of Christ* was shown in an Albuquerque high school, while the Genesis Project's *Jesus* film, whose script is all Scripture, would not be allowed near school grounds.[7]

This is how the neutrality game is played: Christian, you remain neutral so we humanists can implement our version of what's right and wrong, and then we will compel you to live under our set of rules. The state becomes the agent of reform for those who champion the neutrality theory for everyone but themselves. It's no wonder that Harvey Cox described secular humanism as "a dangerous ideological system because it 'seeks to impose its ideology through the organs of the State.'" According to Cox, "secular humanism has no tolerance and is opposed to other religions; it actively rejects, excludes and attempts to eliminate traditional theism from meaningful participation in the American culture."[8]

Neutrality Illogic

According to a recent radio editorial, "a man's religion and the strength of his conviction are his own personal matter," and therefore "religion should not interfere with politics."[9] Of course, this too is an expression of humanist neutrality designed to silence Christians but allow for every other conceivable worldview to find expression in the public arena.

Let's apply humanist neutrality logic to Germany in the 1930s and '40s. Should the churches have remained neutral? Some of them did to the detriment of the Jews and the church of the Lord Jesus Christ. The Confessional Church:

> opposed the Nazification of the Protestant churches, rejected the Nazi racial theories and denounced the anti-Christian doctrines of Rosen-

berg and other Nazi leaders. *In between lay the majority of Protestants, who seemed too timid to join either of the two warring groups, who sat on the fence and eventually, for the most part, landed in the arms of Hitler, accepting his authority to intervene in church affairs and obeying his commands without open protest.*[10]

Those who "sat on the fence," having fallen for the neutrality myth, supported Hitler by default. While they did not openly join with the "German Christians," a pro-Hitler alliance of ministers and churches, their inaction landed them "in the arms of Hitler."

"For a Christian to adopt the neutrality myth is to think like a humanist."

Would the above radio commentator have uttered that "a man's religion and the strength of his conviction are his own personal matter," and "religion should not interfere with politics" if these convictions were used to oppose Hitler and his evil plots against the Jews? Would he have said the same thing to William Wilberforce who, as a member of the British Parliament, worked and succeeded in abolishing the slave trade in England?

Our humanist friends are selective in their assessment of the application of religion to contemporary life, including politics. Our own nation faced a crisis over slavery. Would the humanist guardians of neutrality want to propose that religious leaders should have remained silent (neutral) on the slavery issue? I doubt it.

Birds of a Feather . . .

So then, for a Christian to adopt the neutrality myth is to think like a humanist, to believe that religious convictions are reserved for the heart, home, and place of worship, while the affairs of this world are

best handled by using reason, experience, and technical expertise devoid of religious assumptions and convictions.

> Secular humanists have no objection to our Christian faith at all, pro-
> vided we reserve it strictly for ourselves in the privacy of our homes
> and church buildings, and just as long as we do not try to live up to
> our Christ principles in our business and *public* life. On no account
> must the Spirit and Word of the Lord Jesus Christ be allowed to enter
> the ballot booth or the market place where the real decisions of mod-
> ern life are made, nor must religion interfere with such vital matters
> as education, politics, labor relations and profits and wages. These ac-
> tivities are all supposed to be "neutral" and they can therefore be
> withdrawn from sectarian influences so that the secular spirit of the
> community may prevail.[11]

Humanists and, unfortunately, a majority of Christians believe that
the world's problems can be solved through technical know-how without any regard for divine intervention. This view teaches that special
revelation has little or nothing to say about "secular" things like education, politics, and law. The unbeliever, it is maintained, is capable,
without Scripture, of developing equitable laws, a sound educational
philosophy, and a just political system. This is the myth of neutrality.

Since experience (not to mention the Bible) tells us that there is
no neutrality, we must assume that some philosophy will dominate the
public policy playing field. For Christians to claim "neutrality" is to give
all opposing ideologies a free rein in public policy decision making. "If
religious-based values are not dominant, some other beliefs will be."[12]
Jesus requires Christians to be "the salt of the earth" and the "light of
the world," which means "we must interact with—and influence—public institutions." The Christian's responsibilities in the political order
are prayer, obedience, and using "Scriptural principles to shape public
policy."[13] Neutrality is not an option.

6

"JESUS WAS NOT A SOCIAL REFORMER"

It is exceedingly strange that any followers of Jesus Christ should ever have needed to ask whether social involvement was their concern, and that controversy should have blown up over the relationship between evangelism and social responsibility. For it is evident that in his public ministry Jesus both "went about . . . teaching . . . and preaching" (Matthew 4.23; 9.35 RSV) and "went about doing good and healing" (Acts 10.38 RSV).

JOHN STOTT

During the Easter season in the Philippines, people carry out crucifixions, following Jesus' example. These men could make the case that they are only doing what Jesus did. Of course, few, if any, follow Jesus' example in every detail! Few, if any, die. And as far as I know, no one has been raised from the dead after three days. There are many things that Jesus didn't do. Jesus is unique, and the work He came to earth to accomplish was also unique. In addition, there are a number of things that Jesus did do that we are not to do. Being crucified is one of them.

Let's suppose that we follow Jesus' example regarding marriage and children. Jesus did not get married. Are we to follow His example and abstain from marriage? Of course, having children would be out of the question, too. But we know that Jesus blessed the institution of marriage by performing His first miracle at a wedding in Cana (John 2:1–11) and by giving instructions on the marriage relationship. He enjoins couples to remain married based on one of the Bible's earliest commands: "That He who created them from the beginning made them male and female, and said, 'For this cause a man shall leave his father and mother, and shall cleave to his wife; and the two shall become one flesh'" (Matthew 19:5–6).

The Catholic Church has followed the example of Jesus regarding the marital status of its priests. Why does the Catholic priest take his vow of singleness and celibacy? The primary reason is to imitate Jesus Christ who was unmarried. But some claim additional reasons. "The four Gospels show that Jesus was unmarried so that he could be free to be poor and to preach his message. He had nowhere to lay his head. He was a street rabbi. He lived on handouts, and he was even buried in a borrowed grave."[1] The author misses the key to the biblical witness of Jesus' ministry. Jesus did not remain unmarried so He could be free to be poor and to preach His message. Rather, Jesus' singleness was related to His unique nature and mission. He was God who became man. Jesus' mission was to save His people from their sins, not to be a model husband and father. He performed His unique duty by shedding His blood on a cross, rising from the dead, and ascending to His Father's right hand where He now rules the world.

Jesus never owned a house: "The foxes have holes, and the birds of the air have nests; but the Son of Man has nowhere to lay His head" (Matthew 8:20). And yet, Jesus never condemned the possession of property by rightful owners even though He had no money to pay even the smallest tax. Peter had to fish for a coin to satisfy the requirement to pay the temple tax (Matthew 17:24-27). Based on these two examples, Christians should give all their money away to non-Christians (since, by Jesus' example, Christians cannot possess money) and never own a house.

Again, by following Jesus' example, Christians have the authority to take possession of other people's property because of need. Jesus told

His disciples that if anyone asked why they were taking a donkey and a colt, they were to say, "The Lord has need of them" (Matthew 21:3).

Centuries ago the church debated the issue of using Jesus as an example for ministry. The Spiritualists of the fourteenth century, a sect of the Franciscan Order, "contended eagerly for the view that Christ and his apostles had possessed absolutely nothing, either separately or jointly. This proposition had been declared heretical in a trial before an inquisitor."[2] If Jesus and His apostles possessed nothing (an indefensible claim), then those who take up the gospel ministry must follow their example. St. Francis of Assisi made poverty and celibacy mandatory for all who would join his order.

> This the rule and way of life of the Brothers Minor: to observe the holy gospel of our Lord Jesus Christ, living in obedience, without personal belongings and in chastity. . . .
> The brothers shall possess nothing, neither a house, nor a place, nor anything. But, as pilgrims and strangers in this world, serving God in poverty and humility, they shall continually seek alms, and not be ashamed, for the Lord made himself poor in this world for us.[3]

Jesus and the other New Testament writers made no such demand on the apostles or the church in general (1 Corinthians 7:2–4).[4] We know that the apostles, and the brothers of the Lord, and Peter had a right to take along a believing wife on their missionary journeys (1 Corinthians 9:5).

In addition, Paul defends the right to expect that those who labor in the gospel ministry should receive financial remuneration for their efforts: "If we sowed spiritual things in you, is it too much if we should reap material things from you?" (v. 11). In none of his discussion does Paul refer to Jesus as an example to follow when it comes to marital status or economic position. Rather, he turns the attention of his readers to analogies from everyday life and the Law of Moses (vv. 8–9; Deuteronomy 25:4).

A Higher Principle?

All Scripture is authoritative, not just the words and examples of Jesus. Jesus told His disciples that when the scribes and Pharisees sit in the seat of Moses, that is, when they speak true to Moses, they should do and observe all that the scribes and Pharisees tell them to do (Matthew 23:2–3). Moses, that is, the Old Testament, is authoritative. This is why Paul describes Scripture as being inspired or "God-breathed" (2 Timothy 3:16). The entire New Testament is equally authoritative.

Some want to conclude that while the Old Testament is filled with admonitions for involvement in what are now described as social issues, New Testament believers, because of an obligation to a new and higher principle, are not to involve themselves with social issues and politics. The prophets of the Old Testament spoke out boldly against all types of social injustice. The New Testament seems strangely silent. There are a number of reasons for this supposed silence.

The Absence of Rights Among Captives

How would Christians who were imprisoned in the Gulag be involved in social issues, especially politics? Such a task would have been impossible and even foolhardy. For the most part, prior to the fall of most of Eastern Europe's Communist governments, Christians behind the Iron Curtain had little say in the way their nation operated. This was true of nearly all citizens. Christians were specifically singled out for persecution.[5]

In the Soviet Union, for example, Christians were forbidden to "set up benefit societies, cooperatives of industrial societies; to offer material aid to [their] members; to organize children's and young persons' groups for prayer and other purposes, or general biblical, literary or handicraft groups for the purpose of work or religious instruction and the like, or to organize groups, circles, or sections; to arrange excursions and kindergartens, open libraries and reading rooms, organize sanatoria or medical aid."[6] There is little possibility for social reform under such repressive conditions. One might even make the case that the Russian church's *lack* of social involvement had a part to play in the 1917 revolution.

> It is a sad but irrefutable fact that the Russian Orthodox Church at the time of the Bolshevik Revolution was engaged in a fruitless attempt to preserve its religious treasures (chalices, vestments, paintings,

icons, etc.) and was therefore unable to relate meaningfully to the tremendous social upheavals then taking place.[7]

In a nation under repressive domination, the most immediate need of the Christian community is Christian literature, worship, prayer, and

---

"Christians were at the forefront of many of the efforts to topple communism and bring about reform. When they had an opportunity to institute reforms, they took it."

---

keeping their efforts secret, not social reform that has little chance of success.

Once the Iron Curtain fell, we learned that Christians were at the forefront of many of the efforts to topple communism and bring about reform. When they had an opportunity to institute reforms, they took it. Laszlo Tokes, the Hungarian pastor who sparked the Romanian revolution, stated that "Eastern Europe is not just in a political revolution but a religious renaissance."[8] Instead of being executed, Tokes believed he was saved through divine intervention. The reports that reached the western news media recounted "references to 'Jesus,' the 'Christian spirit,' and Czechoslovakia's role as the 'spiritual crossroads of Europe.'"[9] It was not enough for these Christians to be free to worship. They also wanted to participate in every facet of their nation's life. The church in Czechoslovakia did not take a hands-off approach to social issues once the Iron Curtain began to fall. The Christian leadership saw it as their duty to bring effectual change to the broader culture.

A similar situation existed with Israel under Roman domination. Israel was a captive nation under judgment with little or no voice in Roman affairs. The Jews showed their true allegiance and the reason they were being occupied by a foreign power when they cried out in

Pilate's court when their Messiah was presented to them: "We have no king but Caesar" (John 19:15). This earthly king claimed much more. The inscription on the tribute coin given to Jesus (Matthew 22:15–22) read:

> "TI[berius] CAESAR DIVI AUG[usti] F[ilius] AUGUSTUS," or, in translation, "Tiberius Caesar Augustus, son of the deified Augustus." The inscription was virtually an ascription of deity to the reigning emperor. . . . The irritating presence of the coin was a constant reminder to the Jews of their subservient condition.[10]

The first-century church was born in this era of political oppression and suffered the same social, religious, and political indignities. While Christians were treated cordially by the Roman government for a time, it was not too long before persecution reached a fever pitch. Nero blamed the Christians for the burning of Rome. "[T]he Christians were covered with tar and set up in the imperial parks as living torches, while their women were shamelessly exhibited in mythological pantomimes before being devoured by wild bulls."[11] In fact, the Soviet Union borrowed much from Roman domination tactics. Nikita Khrushchev stated that "When Stalin says dance, the wise man dances!"[12] This echoes the voice of the Beast, Nero Caesar,[13] who decrees that only those who are marked with his name can buy or sell (Revelation 13:11–18). Reforms are impossible under such conditions.

> The deepest reason why the early Christians had less to say about the future of earthly society than had the prophets of Israel was not their mistaken foreshortening of its period, but the fact that they had no present voice or vote in the general affairs of that society. St. Paul addressed his epistles to little groups of men and women who were endeavoring to live the true Christian life in the midst of a vast and powerful, but wholly alien and pagan, society and suited what he had to say to their current needs and problems. It is therefore unfair to expect from these epistles a direct answer to the further questions which inevitably suggest themselves to the mind, because they arise out of the circumstances, of those who like ourselves possess both voice and vote and have accordingly as much responsibility as anybody else for the human direction of affairs of the res publica terrena.[14]

Israel could not act in civil cases until permission was granted by the provincial government of Rome. The elders of Israel had biblical authority to execute capital offenders, but not while they were under the domination of Rome. Although there were times when Rome

---

"In time . . . Rome lost its grip on the world, and Christians began replacing the corrupt courts of paganism with a biblical system of justice."

---

seemed to have looked the other way when Israel decided to take the law into its own hands (Acts 7:60; 14:19), the Pharisees brought Jesus to Pilate because they were "not permitted to put any one to death" (John 18:31).

In time, however, Rome lost its grip on the world, and Christians began replacing the corrupt courts of paganism with a biblical system of justice (1 Corinthians 6:1–11). We should be reminded that the rallying cry of the early church was "Jesus is Lord" (Acts 16:31). The Roman provincial authorities would not have been concerned with what they considered to be a Jewish sect (Acts 24:5, 14) as long as these "Christians" (Acts 11:26) had maintained that Jesus was *a* Lord, subservient to the Roman Emperor and acknowledging his ultimate lordship.

At first, Christianity was perceived as a threat solely to the Jewish leadership. In time, however, Christianity became a threat to Rome because of the implications of absolute lordship: "These men who have upset the world have come here also; . . . and they all act contrary to the decrees of Caesar, saying that there is another king, Jesus" (Acts 17:6–7). You cannot serve two masters. If Jesus is indeed Lord and King (Revelation 19:16), then even Caesar would have to bow before Him

(Philippians 2:9–11; Matthew 2:1–18). The emperors saw the consistency in this view.

God Has Already Spoken

There is a second reason why Jesus and Paul apparently did not lay down a social agenda. Since Jesus and Paul spoke out of a Jewish background and context, direct allusions to political and economic ideologies may have been unnecessary. "Christians must understand that their faith is rooted in Old Testament Judaism and that the Mosaic Covenant and Law (which contain highly specific political, economic, judicial, and social precepts) can give guidance even today."[15] This is why Paul could write that "*all* Scripture is inspired by God" (2 Timothy 3:16, emphasis added). Paul had the Old Testament in mind since the New Testament had not been completed and compiled. There was no need for Jesus or Paul to repeat principles that had already been laid down in great detail in the books of what we now call the Old Testament, what the Bible itself describes simply as Scripture.

There is one further reason why Jesus did not set Himself up as a social reformer. What office would He have sought? Scripture says that He is "King of kings, and Lord of lords" (Revelation 19:5). Jesus was born a king (John 18:37). His position of King and Creator superseded all earthly titles and positions. Reformation would take place in the hearts and minds of those whom He would call to Himself. He would then expect them to live their lives as new creatures who would faithfully work out the implications of their new life in terms of what was set forth in Scripture.

A Negative Example

While Jesus was looked upon as a positive example of why Christians should not be involved in social issues, the Pharisees are seen as negative examples for noninvolvement. The general impression is "the Pharisees were the best people of their day; and yet they were the greatest failures."[16]

The Pharisees were *not* the best people of their day. The best people were men like Simeon (Luke 2:25), Zacharias (Luke 1:6), and Joseph (Matthew 1:19), and women like Anna (Luke 2:36–37), Mary (Luke 1:46–56), and Elizabeth (Luke 1:6). Elizabeth and Zacharias "were both righteous in the sight of God, walking blamelessly in all the command-

---

"The whole Bible has been given for the whole of life. There are numerous admonitions for reform."

---

ments and requirements of the Lord" (Luke 1:6). The commandments of God were neglected by the Pharisees (Mark 7:8). They "nicely set aside the commandment of God in order to keep [their] tradition" (Mark 7:9). Jesus told the Pharisees that they had the devil as their father (John 8:44). James B. Jordan sets the record straight:

> We are used to thinking of the scribes and Pharisees as meticulous men who carefully observed the jots and tittles [of God's law]. This is not the portrait found in the Gospels. The scribes and Pharisees that Jesus encountered were grossly, obviously, and flagrantly breaking the Mosaic law, while keeping all kinds of man-made traditions. Jesus' condemnation of them in Matthew 23 certainly makes this clear, as does a famous story in John 8. There we read that the scribes and Pharisees brought to Jesus a woman taken "in the very act" of adultery (John 8:1–11). How did they know where to find her? Where was the man who was caught with her? Apparently he was one of their cronies. Also, when Jesus asked for anyone "without sin" (that is, not guilty of the same crime) to cast the first stone, they all went away, because they were all adulterers.[17]

A persistent belief beleaguers the church because the Pharisees have been portrayed as strict adherents to the law, and Jesus had His greatest theological disputes with the Pharisees; therefore, Jesus was opposed to the law. This is not what the Bible teaches. When the "scribes and the Pharisees . . . seated themselves in the chair of Moses," that is, when the law was properly taught and applied, the people were to do all that they told them (Matthew 23:2–3). At the same time, Jesus admonished the people "do not do according to their deeds" (23:3).

In the same way, Christians today must listen to all of God's Word, not just the example of Jesus or the negative example of the Pharisees. The whole Bible has been given for the whole of life. There are numerous admonitions for reform: from education to caring for the poor; from ensuring just weights and measures to seeing that there is equal justice for all. The power of the gospel and the work of the Holy Spirit in the lives of God's people can be a great instrument of reform in the world.

"THE CHURCH SHOULD NOT BE INVOLVED IN SOCIAL ISSUES"

It is not the judgments of the courts, but rather the moral judgments of the masses of men and women which constitute the chief defense of life and property. It is public opinion that moulds our laws and institutions; and one of the greatest forces for moulding this opinion has been the church with its Bible. In fact, Christianity is today the most deep-seated and powerful influence in its formation. Thus it is that Christian principles, by slow degrees, are helping toward divine justice as the fundamental basis of all human law.

P. MARION SIMMS

To the pulpit, the *PURITAN PULPIT*, we owe the moral force which won our Independence."[1] Ministers of the gospel confronted the issues of their day by appealing to the people in terms of the Bible. The annual "election sermon" still "bears witness that our fathers ever began their civil year and its responsibilities with an appeal to Heaven, and recognized *Christian morality as the only basis of good laws.*"[2]

In addition, the clergy were often consulted by the civil authorities in the colonies, "and not infrequently the suggestions from the pulpit, on election days and other special occasions, were enacted into laws. The statute-book, the reflex of the age, shows this influence. *The State was developed out of the Church.*"[3]

There were some ministers, however, who refrained from appealing to the Bible for examples and prescriptions for reform. The Rev. Nathaniel Ward (c. 1578—1652), pastor at Ipswich, Massachusetts, in his election sermon of June 1641, grounded "his propositions much upon the Old Roman and Grecian governments." John Winthrop (1588–1649), first governor of Massachusetts, described this as "an error." There was good reason for Winthrop's objection: Why should the church appeal to "heathen commonwealths" when it is the heathen principles that have made it necessary for the church to be involved in reform efforts? Winthrop believed that "religion and the word of God make men wiser than their neighbors," thus, "*we* may better *form rules of government for ourselves*" than to adopt the failed principles of the past, what he called "the bare authority of the wisdom, justice, etc., of those heathen commonwealths."[4] The heathen past had to be swept clean if the people of God were to become the model of Christian charity that Winthrop spoke about aboard the flagship *Arabella* in 1630. Such a task is no less true in our day.

What follows is a very brief study of the emphasis of Christian reform efforts throughout the church's history. While the church has not been perfect in its efforts, there is no doubt that the existing social structure, what is often described as Christian civilization, has been the result of Christian efforts to bring the "whole purpose of God" (Acts 20:27) to bear on the whole of life.

Reform Through the Ages

The first-century church had to live within the confines of the existing laws of the Roman empire. The Apostle Paul had to confront the Roman institution of slavery when he led a runaway slave, Onesimus, to Jesus Christ (Philemon 10). Should Paul have called for the abolition of slavery by petitioning the Roman government to abolish the slave trade? Should the apostle have encouraged Onesimus to lead a rebellion against the Roman slaveholders and ultimately against the Roman gov-

---

"The existing social structure . . . has been the result of Christian efforts to bring the 'whole purpose of God' to bear on the whole of life."

---

ernment? Should Paul have remained silent on the issue, claiming that it was not the responsibility of the church to involve itself in social reform?

As we've already noted, the church was in no position to petition the Roman government to do much of anything, let alone release millions of slaves that were vital to the Roman way of life. There was little that Israel could do, even when faced with the murder of infants (Matthew 2:16).

> No formal protest is recorded as having been registered with the king, and no action violating accepted civic law is reported. It may have been that the action was taken too rapidly to allow organized protest. But it seems more likely that any protest of citizenry would have been quickly suppressed by the Roman state.[5]

The historian Edward Gibbon estimates that there were more than sixty million slaves in the Roman Empire of the first century. Other writers place their estimates even higher. Tacitus, a Roman historian of the first century, writes that the "city of Rome was in constant fear of an uprising of the slaves. When a measure was proposed in the senate to have all slaves dress alike to distinguish them from freemen, the suggestion was promptly killed by the argument that to do so would reveal to the slaves their great numerical strength and endanger the peace of the city by a possible revolt."[6]

No Legal Standing

Jews had few civil rights compared to Roman citizens (Acts 22:22–29), and slaves had none at all. Roman law gave masters nearly absolute power to sell, exchange, seize for debt, or kill a slave at will. "Slaves had no legal standing in the courts, no legal parentage, no right to hold property, and no civil rights. When compelled to testify in the courts their depositions were legal only when taken under torture."[7] Slaves were treated worse than cattle:

> In ancient times slavery was widespread. Especially among the Greeks it was common practice to reduce captives and often criminals and debtors to the state of bondage. On the island of Delos sometimes as many as ten thousand slaves were sold in a single day. Among the Romans the lot of the slave seems to have been more cruel than among the Greeks. The slave was not considered to have any rights. The law offered him no protection.[8]

If a slave killed his master, all of the slaves in his household could be put to death. Tacitus relates an incident where the revolt of one slave against his master resulted in the death of about six hundred household slaves.

Paul did not remain silent on the slavery issue. He worked for lasting reform by dealing with Christian brethren who would in the future influence the Roman government and the institution of slavery directly. In time, slavery would be abolished without revolution. Revolution rarely, if ever, brings lasting reform. Once the cycle of revolution begins, there is little that can be done to stop it.

Legal Emancipation

As a runaway slave, Onesimus would have had little chance of survival in the Roman world. He would have lacked the necessary papers to travel and work. Paul instructed him to return to his master Philemon. Paul understood that social reform must flow from personal reform. The advocation of revolution to bring about reformation is an unbiblical idea. Philemon had to be convinced that slavery was wrong before an appreciable change could take lasting effect. Many other Christians had to be equally convinced that slavery was wrong before it could be abolished. By going back to his master, Onesimus could be legally emancipated and thus enjoy the same rights as other free men without civil repercussions.

It is quite evident from other New Testament passages that slavery, as it was practiced by the Greeks and Romans, was abhorrent to God. Kidnappers—"slave-dealers"—are denounced along with murderers and sodomites (1 Timothy 1:9–10). The Old Testament view of slavery is quite different from that practiced by Greece, Rome, and in the United States prior to 1860. Biblical slavery was designed for a convicted thief who was unable to make restitution for his crime (Exodus 22:1–3). Bad debts were often paid through a form of indentured servitude (Deuteronomy 15), a practice that the United States Constitution retained even after the abolition of slavery: "Neither slavery nor involuntary servitude, *except as a punishment for crime whereof the party shall have been duly convicted,* shall exist within the United States, or any place subject to their jurisdiction" (Amendment XIII, Section 1, emphasis added).

Although other types of slavery existed in Israel, none of them resembled the Roman institution.[9] For the Hebrew indentured servant the seventh year was the year of emancipation (Exodus 21:1–2). If the jubilee year arrived before the seventh year, then in that year freedom was granted (Leviticus 25:39–41). Cruelty was never permitted (Exodus 21:26–27). Slavery as "man stealing," the type of slavery practiced in Greece, Rome, England, and the United States, would not have been permitted under biblical law: "And he who kidnaps [literally, steals] a man, whether he sells him or he is found in his possession, shall surely be put to death" (Exodus 21:16).

As far as we know, Philemon was not a slave trader. He owned at least one slave like countless other Roman citizens, although we do not know the reason for Onesimus's servitude. Onesimus could have been an indentured servant who was repaying a debt. In any case, Paul was taking the first steps in setting forth a doctrine of social reform regarding a practice that was common and accepted in the Roman world. He was far ahead of his time by working with Christians who were slave owners to develop an equitable and nondisruptive arrangement for the emancipation of their slaves.

Jesus Sets the Pattern

Jesus established the precedent for the abolition of slavery when he declared the *"fulfillment of the provisions of the jubilee year"* (Luke 4:16–21, emphasis added).[10]

> Christianity did not inaugurate a violent crusade against slavery. To have commanded and attempted the immediate overthrow of slavery in the Roman Empire would probably have wrought great havoc, brought greater burdens and suffering upon the unfortunate slaves, plunged masters and slaves into protracted war, and turned Europe and Asia into fields of blood.[11]

The Apostle Paul built on the theological foundation for emancipation laid by Jesus when he wrote that in Christ Jesus "there is neither slave nor free man" (Galatians 3:28). Emancipation would have to come through reconciliation in Jesus Christ where the slave could be regarded as a brother. This was Paul's admonition to Philemon, that he would receive Onesimus back to him "no longer as a slave, but more than a slave, a beloved brother" (Philemon 16).

The message of freedom made its way slowly through the church and empire. In time, however, Rome would be judged by God for trafficking in slaves. Those "kings of the earth, who committed acts of immorality" (Revelation 18:9) would come under the judgment of God (v. 10) because of their buying and selling of "slaves and human lives" (v. 13).

The sad fact is that it took centuries before the church became the reforming institution that Jesus and Paul intended it to be in the area of emancipation. It's true that "multitudes of slaves were received into the Christian brotherhood," and "under the reign of Hadrian, 117–138, the law forbade the arbitrary killing of a slave and granted the right of trial to establish innocence or guilt." In addition,

> under Constantine, 312–337, and the succeeding emperors further legislation relieved their conditions. . . . Further legislation to improve conditions of the slaves was enacted under Justinian, 527–567. All privileges accorded to citizens were granted to emancipated slaves.
>
> One great benefit to slaves, rendered by Christianity, was the recognition of the marriage-tie as valid and indissoluble. . . . Under the influence of Christianity much favorable legislation was secured, many

burdens lightened, many abuses righted, and more humane treatment secured.[12]

Nearly 1800 years passed before full emancipation of slaves was championed by the church, although there were pockets of reform efforts before total emancipation was realized.

The English Abolition Movement

Generally, the Christian community in England supported slavery. An example of this blindness can be seen in the career of John Newton (1725–1807). Newton was an infamous slave trader. The church knows him best as the author of such well-known hymns as "Amazing Grace" and "Glorious Things of Thee Are Spoken." Newton's opposition to

---

> **"England's abolition movement was almost entirely led by the evangelical wing of the church."**

---

slavery did not develop until *after* he became a Christian. Even while Newton was still a Christian he was also a captain of a slave ship. "Newton penned the beloved hymn 'How Sweet the Name of Jesus Sounds in a Believer's Ear' during the leisure time afforded by a voyage from Africa to the West Indies."[13]

In time, however, Newton confessed "shame" for "the misery and mischief to which [he had], formerly, been accessory." He eventually denounced his former occupation with the publication of *Thoughts Upon the African Slave Trade* (1788), "a stinging attack upon slavery that makes scenes from Alex Haley's *Roots* seem mild by comparison."[14] Newton believed, prior to his denunciation of the slave trade, that he could be a good Christian and still participate in a great evil. "By 1788 Newton considered it 'criminal' to remain silent and not inveigh with evangelical fervor against the entire slave system. This conviction did not arise automatically upon his conversion, but from ethical deliberations that [William] Wilberforce set in motion."[15]

England's abolition movement was almost entirely led by the evangelical wing of the church. At the pleading of Lady Middleton and Bishop Porteus, James Ramsay wrote *Essay on the Treatment and and Conversion of Slaves in the British Sugar Colonies* (1784). Ramsay was "convinced that men will not respond to lessons of eternal redemption from those who enslave them on earth, or about heaven when kept in hell. . . . "[16] He proposed steps to total Emancipation, and suggested that free labour would yield more profit to plantation owners.

William Wilberforce, upon being struck with the oppression inherent in the slave trade, wrote in his diary, "Almighty God has set before me two great objectives: The abolition of the slave trade and the reformation of manners."[17] Wilberforce began his mission in 1787. His efforts were ridiculed and lampooned in popular cartoons. "The attitude in the House of Lords was summed up by the member who declared flatly, 'All abolitionists are Jacobins.'"[18] Such an accusation is the modern equivalent of calling someone an anarchist, Bolshevik, Marxist, or revolutionary. A bill outlawing slavery finally passed in 1807. Had the British government "not been in the hands of Christians there seems little reason to have expected it to mount its massive, expensive, and voluntary campaign against slavery."[19]

American Abolition at Great Cost

The past practice of slavery in the United States continues to affect those who were enslaved against their will. Although emancipation has come, it was a long and arduous road. Keep in mind that it wasn't until the 1860s that slavery was constitutionally abolished. John Eliot, "the apostle to the Indians," protested in 1675 against the treatment of captives in King Philip's War. Most of the male captives (including those who voluntarily surrendered) were enslaved and traded to the West Indies for black slaves. Eliot argued that sending the Indians away hindered their conversion to the blessings of Christianity. Eliot was one of the earliest Christians to challenge the slave trade. "This usage of them," Eliot said of the Indian captives, "is worse than death."[20]

Because of the silence, and in many cases the support of slavery, on the part of much of the evangelical wing of the church in the United States, especially in the South, emancipation was won only at great

---

"The New Testament church was involved in all types of reform efforts, with widows and orphans receiving special care."

---

cost. The task of liberating slaves was left to radicals and terrorists. America is still paying a heavy price for the unrighteous way blacks were treated and the way they were emancipated.

If modern antireformists had their way, the institution of slavery would still be with us. They would be preaching to the church to remain silent on the issue since, in their way of thinking, the church should not be involved in social issues.

The Bible as the "Magna Carta" of the Poor and Oppressed

As we have seen, the church has been in the forefront of establishing political freedom as in the antislavery crusade in England. In addition, there is a long tradition of the establishment of schools and hospitals around the globe. Medical and educational missionary work has its origins in the evangelical struggle for reform. Great efforts of social reform followed the preaching of the gospel. "Historians have attributed to [John] Wesley's influence rather than to any other the fact that Britain was spared the horrors of a bloody revolution like France's."[21] His philosophy of social reform was derived from the Bible.

Caring for the Poor and Infirm

The New Testament church was involved in all types of reform efforts, with widows and orphans receiving special care. "The English philosopher Sir Francis Bacon (1561–1626) declared that 'there never was found, in any age of the world, either religion or law that did so highly exalt the public good as the Bible.'"[22] Scripture set forth policies to care for the poor, widows, orphans, and strangers (Deuteronomy 14:28–29). Landowners were obligated to set aside a portion of their harvested fields for the less fortunate (Leviticus 19:9) for purposes of gleaning (Leviticus 23:22). The remaining sheaves were to be left for the poor (Deuteronomy 24:19), while the crops that grew of themselves were to remain unharvested in the seventh year as a way of helping the poor (Exodus 23:10–11).[23] Thomas Huxley noted and paid tribute to the advanced social thinking reflected in the Pentateuch:

> The Bible has been the Magna Carta of the poor and of the oppressed; down to modern times no State has had a constitution in which the interests of the people are so largely taken into account, in which the duties so much more than the privileges of rulers are insisted upon, as that drawn up for Israel in Deuteronomy and Leviticus; nowhere is the fundamental truth that the welfare of the State, in the long run, depends on the uprightness of the citizen so strongly laid down.[24]

The Old Testament commands for social reform in helping the poor, especially widows and orphans, were not lost on the New Testament writers. Relief efforts were immediately taken up by the early church to care for the widows who "were being overlooked in the daily serving of food" (Acts 6:1; 1 Timothy 5:8–10). Furthermore, when it was learned that there would be "a great famine all over the world," the disciples, "in the proportion that any of [them] had means, each of them determined to send a contribution for the relief of the brethren living in Judea" (Acts 11:28–29).

The church continued the biblical tradition of reform as it grew in number and influence. The relief of the poor was always high on the list. Caring for the infirm fell to the church as well. "Take, for example, the way Christians tried to help afflicted fellow Christians and pagans alike during the mid-third-century plague. Dionysius, bishop of Alexandria, described his flock's activities as 'visiting the sick without a thought as to the danger, assiduously ministering to them, tending them in Christ.'"[25] Cotton Mather (1663–1728) had an abiding interest in medical matters. "When a small pox epidemic threatened Boston he proposed to the local physicians that they practice the method [of inoculation] and save the town."[26]

It is no accident that many hospitals carry the names of churches: Lutheran General, Christ, Mercy Hospital, Presbyterian-St. Luke's, Swedish Covenant, and dozens more. Jewish, Roman Catholic, and Eastern Orthodox have a prestigious tradition of social reform in the area of medicine. Mather, in his *Essays to Do Good* (1710), "proposed that men and women, acting either as individuals or as members of voluntary associations, should engage in 'a perpetual endeavor to do good in the world.'"[27]

Caring for the Dispossessed

As Christians gained influence and positions of authority, reform efforts expanded. Abortion, infanticide, and the abandonment of children were common practices in Roman society. Many parents considered children a burden. If they did not leave them to die from exposure, they would leave them in public places provided for abandonment. "Occasionally benevolent persons might rescue such children. Sometimes witches would take them and use their bodies for incantations. Some of them died from exposure, while the majority were taken and reared by lewd persons and finally sold as slaves or prostitutes."[28] The reform efforts of Christians changed all of this.

> The Church councils, Christian emperors, and lawmakers sought by declarations and legislation to combat the crime. As early as 323 the Council of Nice decreed that hospitals should be established in the chief cities and towns, and exhorted that these hospitals should make provision to take care of abandoned children.
>
> Houses of Mercy were provided by the Church for these foundlings. A marble vessel was placed at each church to receive exposed infants. These children were sometimes adopted by members. Those not cared

for by some private family were taken under the charge of the Church.[29]

The evils of abortion and infanticide were also an accepted part of Roman society. Some laws prohibiting the practices were instituted by the pagan emperors, but the measures were rarely if ever enforced. Laws banning abortion and infanticide came into being because it was Christianity that sought to establish the dignity and value of all human beings, even the unborn. It has only been since the early 1970s that this Christian tradition of reform regarding the protection of the unborn has been overturned.

"Just Preach the Gospel"

A number of Christian leaders would want to maintain that the church's job is to "just preach the gospel." Indeed it is. But aren't there implications to the gospel message? Jesus and the New Testament writers certainly thought so. Jesus said that you will know a converted person by the fruit his profession produces (Matthew 7:15–23). A profession of faith does not validate a person's conversion. James tells us that faith without works is dead (James 2:14–26). Prior to this, he tells us "This is pure and undefiled religion in the sight of our God and Father, to visit orphans and widows in their distress, and to keep oneself unstained by the world" (James 1:27).

Maybe the advocates of "just preaching the gospel" have a limited understanding of what the gospel is all about. Paul told the Ephesian elders that he did not shrink from declaring to them the "whole purpose of God" (Acts 20:27). A reading of Paul's letters to the churches will show that he spent as much time on Christian behavior after conversion as he did on correct doctrine. He wrote about the "renewing of your mind." Certainly an application can be made to education, entertainment, and reading material since we are not to be "conformed to this world." Paul also discusses such "secular" issues as "contributing to the needs of the saints" (our duty to the church) and the ministry of civil government, including paying taxes "to whom tax is due" (our duty to the state) (Romans 12:2, 13; 13:7). But politics is one area where many Christians want to draw the line:

> It is hoped that but a few will think the subject of [civil government] an improper one to be discussed on in the pulpit, under a notion that this is *preaching politics,* instead of Christ. However, to remove all prejudices of this sort, I beg it may be remembered that "all Scripture is profitable for doctrine, for reproof, for correction, for instruction in righteousness" [2 Timothy 3:16]. Why, then, should not those parts of Scripture which relate to *civil government* be examined and explained from the desk, as well as others. Obedience to the civil magistrate is a Christian duty; and if so, why should not the nature, grounds, and extent of it be considered in a Christian assembly? Besides, if it be said that it is out of character for a Christian minister to meddle with such a subject, this censure will at last fall upon the holy apostles. They write upon it in their epistles to Christian churches; and surely it cannot be deemed either criminal or impertinent to attempt an explanation of their doctrine.[30]

Mayhew's point is well taken. If the writers of Scripture, as instruments of God's will (2 Timothy 3:16), did not think it improper to

---

"It was Christianity that sought to establish the dignity and value of all human beings, even the unborn."

---

discuss political issues, then how can ministers who claim allegiance to an inspired and infallible Bible fail to address not only politics but every issue discussed in Scripture?

Paul repeats the commandments prohibiting adultery, murder, and theft and sums up his specific exhortation on the law with the general command to "love your neighbor as yourself" (Romans 13:9). This commandment alone has multiple social applications. Certainly it is the duty of the civil magistrate to love his neighbor by not burdening him with excessive taxation and bureaucratic entanglements to frustrate his freedoms to earn a living. It seems by all of this that Paul went beyond what many might think of as "just preaching the gospel." You can find similar emphases in all the New Testament letters as well as in the ministry of Jesus.

Revivalism and Social Reform

Ernest Fremont Tittle said "that 'Evangelical religion' could never hope to produce a humane social order."[31] This assertion is impossible to prove when one looks carefully at the evidence. Charles Finney, best known as a revivalist preacher, saw an obvious relationship between evangelism and social reform. John Stott writes about Finney's views:

> Social involvement was both the child of evangelical religion and the twin sister of evangelism. This is clearly seen in Charles G. Finney, who is best known as the lawyer turned evangelist and author of *Lectures on Revivals of Religion* (1835). Through his preaching of the gospel large numbers were brought to faith in Christ. What is not so well known is that he was concerned for "reforms" as well as "revivals." He was convinced . . . both that the gospel "releases a mighty impulse toward social reform" and that the church's neglect of social reform grieved the Holy Spirit and hindered revival. It is astonishing to read Finney's statement in his twenty-third lecture on revival that *"the great business of the church is to reform the world. . . . The Church of Christ was originally organised to be a body of reformers. The very profession of Christianity implies the profession and virtually an oath to do all that can be done for the universal reformation of the world."*[32]

These are remarkable words considering the general evangelical and fundamentalist attitude toward social reform in our day. Most Christians have no idea that a theology of reform was developed by men who are known only as "soul winners." But when we dig a bit deeper into Finney's thought, we soon learn that he too met resistance in his advocation of reform efforts. He was amazed that the church treated "the different branches of reform either with indifference, or with direct opposition." Finney described opposition to reform efforts as "monstrous" and "God-dishonoring."[33] In spite of opposition, however, reforms were realized.

Christianity once saved the world from barbarism by redeeming the pagan civilization of Rome, a decrepit and dying culture. The barbarians are once again loose in the land, not because the barbarians are so formidable but because of the lack of a commitment to social reform by the church. The splendor of these reform efforts of the early church form the backdrop for evangelical works of social reform that swept through our nation in its formative years. These great Christian pioneers have left the church a great legacy. We dare not squander their efforts by preaching a gospel that has no regard for man and his world.

PART 3

THE CHRISTIAN AND POLITICS

8

"POLITICS IS DIRTY"

*Some, unfortunately, think that politics is a
dirty word and a corrupt game that public officials play. In reality, it is the very fabric of
the democratic system of government that
we cherish so much. While it is made up of
people like us who have problems and often
yield to self-interests and lesser motives, it is
still the strength of our society.*

GORDON W. JONES

T hose of you who have children will be able to identify with this
scenario. You hear your five-week-old baby crying. You know
what her problem is. She has a dirty diaper. You know what needs to be
done. Her diaper needs changing. Let's say that Dad comes back after
verifying that it is a dirty diaper and says, "Yes, her diaper's dirty, so I
can't get involved in changing it."

Sounds ridiculous, doesn't it? Dad was sent to change what was
dirty, a natural and necessary thing to do. If this is so foolish, why is it
that when we get to an area like politics, some can justify their inaction
by making a similar claim? "Politics is dirty! I can't get involved."

If you have trouble getting involved in something as dirty as politics, then just look at politics as a large dirty diaper that's in need of
being changed and the body politic as a baby in need of a thorough

cleaning. Maybe then we can dispense with the charge that Christians should not be involved in something as dirty as politics.

Civil Government Is Established by God

Civil government is established by God; therefore, it is a legitimate area of activity for Christians (Matthew 22:21; Romans 13:1; 1 Timothy 2:1–4; 1 Peter 2:13–17). There was a need for civil government when man sinned and became a threat to other men (Genesis 4:23). Politics is the process of electing the best men to office to protect law-abiding citizens against the lawless (Exodus 18; Deuteronomy 1:15; 1 Timothy 3:1–7). Soon after the flood, God formalized civil government by, as Martin Luther wrote, sharing "his power with man" and granting "him power over life and death among men" (Genesis 9:4–6).[1] To speak out against the principle of political involvement is to call God's wisdom into question and to allow the despot to rule.

Civil Government Is One Government Among Many

The political sphere is a created entity like the family and church. "God has instituted civil government just as He has set up the church and the family. To say we want nothing to do with civil government is to say that God's institution is not important."[2] We are created in the image of God. God is the Governor over all creation, and He has called us to be delegated and limited governors under His one, all-embracing, and unlimited government (Isaiah 9:6–7): self-governors, family governors, church governors, and civil governors. The civil or political sphere is an area of legitimate governmental activity that has a designated jurisdiction and set of prescribed biblical laws for its operation. It has its dirty elements when evil men practice evil schemes. But so do other human activities, such as business, law, education, and so forth. It is the result of our sinful human condition.[3]

> The burden of proof is on the one who thinks that the politics of running a government is any more dirty or dishonest than the politics of running a bank, labor union, trucking company, college, or even a

church. Because of its life in a goldfish bowl, the governmental process may actually be a bit cleaner and more honest that the process of running most other social institutions.[4]

Christians should be involved in politics even if it is dirty. God expects Christians to clean up their own lives after their conversion (Acts 26:20). The cleanup process should extend to the family. Re-

---

"To speak out against the principle of political involvement is to call God's wisdom into question and to allow the despot to rule."

---

member, children are to obey their parents in the Lord (Ephesians 6:1). This means sinful attitudes and actions must be substituted with godly attitudes and actions. Husbands are to love their wives (5:25), and wives are to be subject to their husbands (5:22). Certainly the church has the responsibility to get its house in order (1 Peter 4:17). Most of the New Testament epistles were written to churches, some of which had serious problems (1 Corinthians 5:1–8).

This cleanup process does not come naturally. It's a matter of "[cleaning] out the old leaven" (1 Corinthians 5:7). "Let us behave properly as in the day, not in carousing and drunkenness, not in sexual promiscuity and sensuality, not in strife and jealousy. But put on the Lord Jesus Christ, and make no provision for the flesh in regard to its lusts" (Romans 13:13–14). These sinful attitudes and actions are present in all fallen creatures, and they manifest themselves in self-government, family government, church government, and civil government, the realm of politics. Paul's admonition applies to every area where sinful man acts.

The People Make Politics What It Is

It's been said that clothes make the man. In biblical terms we can assert that the character of the people will determine what type of political system a nation gets. Our nation was founded on the belief that religion undergirds the society. "In the last resort, our civilization is what we think and believe. The externals matter, but they cannot stand if the inner convictions which originally produced them have vanished."[5] Dirty (sinful) politics is simply the reflection of sinful men and women—politicians and voters included. In other words, we get what we deserve; we reap what we have sown.

> So when a sleazy candidate gets elected, or when your local newspaper or TV station seems to favor the abortionists, or when a jury in Cincinnati says an abominable set of photographs isn't legally obscene— when any of those things happen, don't leap to the conclusion that someone did a number on us. Consider instead the sober likelihood that the sleazy politician really represents the values of the people who voted, that most subscribers to the paper and those who watch TV really don't care about—or even prefer—abortion, and that precious few jurors are willing to sit in judgment on anything.[6]

Politics is only as good as the people who make it their calling and those who put them into office either by voting or refusing to vote. The maintenance of good government is dependent on good people. George Washington, in his Farewell Address (September 17, 1796), gave this advice to the nation: "Of all the dispositions and habits which lead to political prosperity, religion and morality are indispensable supports."

James Madison, the father and architect of the Constitution, made the connection between self-government and the stability of civilization:

> We have staked the whole future of American civilization, not upon the power of government, far from it. We have staked the future . . . upon the capacity of all of us to govern ourselves, to sustain ourselves, according to the Ten Commandments of God.[7]

No governing document can create freedom, national stability, or security from internal or external forces. The best political intentions are no match for the will of the people. In purely human terms, people are the determiners of the goodness of a nation's political system. John Adams wrote: "Our Constitution was made only for a moral and religious people. It is wholly inadequate to the government of any other."[8]

"Who else has the means to clean [politics] up? If Christians do not, who will?"

When self-government is abandoned for self-serving opportunism, we should expect a decline in the health of the nation. Politics will indeed become dirty.

Dirty Business

Why is politics left out of the cleanup process when politics plays such a significant part in our lives? Who else has the means to clean it up? If Christians do not, who will? Christians have stayed out of politics, making its corruption even more pronounced. The answer is not to consign politics to even more corruption by ignoring its potential as an area for redemption and restoration.

Sports certainly is a dirty business. Ben Johnson of Canada was suspended after his world-record-breaking performance at the 1988 Olympic Games because it was learned that he used performance-enhancing drugs—anabolic steroids. Pete Rose, former player and manager for the Cincinnati Reds, was convicted of income tax evasion and reports of gambling. The gambling was linked to his baseball playing. How many parents will remove their children from participating in sports because of the dirt? The International Olympic Committee has been working hard to clean up those sports where steroids are the drug of choice, especially in track and field and weight lifting. These officials recognize that there is dirt, but they have not abandoned sports because of it.

The Bible and Political Involvement

The Bible never condemns political involvement. John the Baptist does not rebuke Herod for his political position, but for his sinful actions as a ruler (Matthew 14:4; Mark 6:18), and neither does he tell the soldiers to resign their positions. He only exhorts them to act ethically; that is, keep politics clean (Luke 3:14). Jesus does not quarrel with Pontius Pilate over whether he should rule; He only reminds him *why* he rules and, implicitly, by what standard he ought to rule (John 19:11). Again, clean politics is the emphasis. Paul calls rulers God's ministers, servants in the political sphere (Romans 13:4). These rulers are to promote the good. Paul appeals to Caesar, the seat of Roman political power, to gain a hearing for the cause of the gospel (Acts 25:11). Why turn to the civil magistrate for civil protection if the civil government (politics) is inherently evil? How could Paul ask support for the purity of the gospel from something that was inherently "dirty"?

A Presbyterian Conflict

The desire to retreat from political concerns is recent within our nation's history. John Witherspoon, a minister in the Presbyterian church and the president of Princeton College, was a signer of the Declaration of Independence. In 1775 "the new provincial congress of New Jersey . . . was opened with prayer by John Witherspoon. . . . A combatant of skepticism and the narrow philosophy of the materialists, he was deputed by Somerset county to take part in applying his noble theories to the construction of a civil government."[9] Many historians contend that the thirteen colonies would never have broken away from Great Britain if it had not been for the Christians, especially the Presbyterians. An ardent colonial supporter of King George III wrote home:

> I fix all the blame for these extraordinary proceedings upon the Presbyterians. They have been the chief and principal instruments in all these flaming measures. They always do and ever will act against government from the restless and turbulent anti-monarchial spirit which has always distinguished them everywhere.[10]

The Presbyterians, because of their doctrines of multiple civil juris-dictions and interdiction, that is, a lesser magistrate (colonial govern-ment) imposing itself through representatives chosen by the people between the greater magistrate (English Parliament) and the people,

---

"The Bible never condemns political involvement."

---

supported independence from British rule. "Ministers sat on Revolution-ary committees and thousands of Presbyterians hastened to join the Revolutionary forces, where they proved the most steadfast of Washington's soldiers."[11]

The framers of the Constitution, "with no more than five excep-tions (and perhaps no more than three), . . . were orthodox members of one of the established Christian communions: approximately twenty-nine Anglicans, sixteen to eighteen Calvinists, two Methodists, two Lu-therans, two Roman Catholics, one lapsed Quaker and sometime-Angli-can, and one open Deist—Dr. [Benjamin] Franklin, who attended every kind of Christian worship, called for public prayer, and contributed to all denominations."[12]

The reason these Christians got involved in politics was because it was dirty. The dirt was affecting their lives, property, and sacred honor. The church had come under the state's jurisdiction to the detriment of the church. Christians rallied to involve themselves in the political pro-cess to keep the church free from political oppression.

Politics Will Not Save Us

After concluding that politics is a legitimate area for Christian ministry, we should also recognize the danger in seeing politics as our salvation. The people in Gideon's day saw politics as the solution to their im-mediate problems (Judges 8:22–23), when, in fact, they were the problem, every man doing what was right in his own eyes (17:6). If they just had a powerful king to rule over them, their problems would be solved, so they thought. Gideon rejected their overtures to make him their savior-king. "The LORD shall rule over you," was Gideon's response (8:23). Gideon was not asserting that politics was evil. But seeing politics as the means to salvation is.

Later, Abimelech wanted to turn the people back to the political faith (9:1–6). Jotham, the only surviving son of Gideon, warned the people of the inherent dangers in such a move (9:7–15). While there was the offer of political salvation and security, it was an illusion that brought with it a shocking tyranny (9:15).

The choice of the political faith brought with it further oppression. Instead of crying out to God in repentance, the people abandoned personal holiness and opted for a new definition of what ought to be. The corrupted family (Judges 14–16) and priesthood (1 Samuel 2:12–17, 22–36) led the people to turn to the state for salvation (1 Samuel 8). In the process they rejected God as king over them (8:7).

The Christian ought to call politics into question when it promises salvation, not because it is an illegitimate sphere of Christian activity. Politics was never meant to save; it cannot save. While we are to redeem politics and the civil sphere of government, we are never to view them as the sole solution to our nation's problems.

9

"RELIGION AND POLITICS DO NOT MIX"

*1. God only—and never any creature—is
possessed of sovereign rights, in the destiny
of nations, because God alone created them,
maintains them by his almighty power, and
rules them by his ordinances. 2. Sin has, in
the realm of politics, broken down the direct
government of God, and therefore the exercise of authority, for the purpose of government, has subsequently been invested in
men as a mechanical remedy. And 3. In
whatever form this authority may reveal itself, man never possesses power over his fel-
low-man in any other way than by an authority which descends upon him from the
majesty of God.*

ABRAHAM KUYPER

E arly in the nineteenth century, a blasphemer in New York thought
that religion and politics did not mix. "'Nonsense,' ruled Justice
James Kent, 'for the people need religion and morality to bind society
together.' He then added: 'The people of this state, in common with
the people of this country, profess the general doctrines of Christianity

as the rule of their faith and practice.' The decision in this case, the justice concluded, rested upon the incontrovertible fact that we are a Christian people."[1]

While more and more Christians are becoming convinced that the Bible has something to say about *some* social issues, like family and education, where an immediate and personal impact is felt, there are others who still have trouble with a biblical view of economics, law, and—the subject of this chapter—politics. The claim is that the Bible separates politics from religious precepts. Like oil and water, religion and politics are not to mix. When the Bible does address political issues, it only does so in the context of a necessary and unavoidable evil. In this view, politics is more than dirty, it's downright diabolic.

Now, we want to be sure we're understood when we say that religion and politics are interrelated. Certainly we do not mean that civil government (the political or legislative process) should be used to change or reform men and women (though the fear of punishment has a deterrent effect on people who might consider a criminal act). No man, or group of men, "can by any means redeem his brother, or give to God a ransom for him" (Psalm 49:7). The purpose of God's law as it relates to the civil magistrate is to punish and restrain evil, to protect human life and property, and to provide justice for all people. Only God can regenerate the heart. An individual cannot be made good by keeping the law.

The Three Uses of the Law

Traditionally, the law has had three uses: (1) to make sinners aware of their rebellion against God and to drive them to embrace Jesus Christ as Lord and Savior (Galatians 3:24); (2) to serve as a standard of obedience for those in whose heart the Spirit of God lives and rules (John 14:15); and (3) to serve as the standard for the just ordering of all aspects of society, civil government included (Romans 13:3–4).

The Bible exists as the state's perfect standard of justice. When the Bible speaks to civil affairs, civil rulers have a duty to heed its commands. How will rulers determine what is good or evil, unless God's law is consulted? (Romans 13:4). Where God's law is not the standard, there can be no objective gauge for man to follow. Law becomes arbitrary.

A Restraint on Evil

The objection that religion and politics do not mix can be answered in at least three ways. First, it is true that the Bible's primary concern is not politics. Of course, the same could be said about the Bible's emphasis on family, church, and education. And yet, there are few Christians who would maintain that Christians should not be involved in family, church, and educational issues, all areas of vital concern where politics

---

"If the Christian religion cannot mix with politics, that is, if it cannot act as the standard for determining right and wrong, then what standard will be used?"

---

has a direct impact. The political realm invades each of these areas, often leading to excessive control. Political restrictions on private and home schools, for example, put families at the mercy of a bankrupt public education system and a despotic state.

The church is no longer considered a sacrosanct institution. Pastors and churches have been sued for offering counseling and denying admitted homosexuals employment. If the Christian religion cannot mix with politics, that is, if it cannot act as the standard for determining right and wrong, then what standard will be used?

Second, because there is sin in the world, God has created temporal ways of dealing with it. In family government, God has designated mothers and fathers as rulers (governors) to admonish and discipline their children because children tend to disobey their parents (Ephesians 6:1–3). The "rod of correction" is the family's instrument of discipline

(Proverbs 13:24). In the church, depending on the ecclesiastical governmental structure, bishops (Episcopalian), elders (Presbyterian), and
deacons (Congregational) rule. The reason for church government, including its laws and discipline, is the reality of sin even among Christians (1 Corinthians 5–6). Ecclesiastical governors have the authority to
use the "keys of the kingdom" in relation to cases of discipline in the
hope of restoring erring members (Matthew 16:19; 18:15–20).

Third, the state, which is best described as civil government,[2] has
been given authority to maintain order in society, to punish the evil-
doer and to promote the good (Genesis 9:5–6; Romans 13:1–6; 1 Peter
2:13–14).

Politics, then, is not a necessary evil; it's necessary because of evil
(Genesis 4:4–15, 23–24; 9:5–7). The sword is the state's God-ordained
instrument of wrath. Civil government, the realm of politics, is only an
"avenger" for "the one who practices evil" (Romans 13:4). This is why
the "law is not made for a righteous man, but for those who are lawless
and rebellious, for the ungodly and sinners, for the unholy and profane,
for those who kill their fathers or mothers, for murderers and immoral
men and homosexuals and kidnappers and liars and perjurers . . . ." (1
Timothy 1:9–10).

This question remains: What standard will those who rule in the
political realm use to determine how they ought to rule? What makes
one law better than any other law? All law is ultimately religious. Some
religion will be adopted to set the standard for political decision making
similar to the way families and church governments operate.

Some may want to protest by declaring that the domain of politics
is purely secular. This was the opinion of Supreme Court Justice Harry
Blackmun. Writing for the majority in the Allegheny County, Pennsylvania, crèche case, he described America as a "secular nation." A "secular nation" is a nation that goes out of its way to keep religion (usually
Christianity) out of the public arena so it can bring another one in.
Social theorist Herbert Schlossberg observes: "Western society, in turning away from the Christian faith, has turned to other things. This process is commonly called *secularization*, but that conveys only the negative aspect. The word connotes the turning away from the worship of
God while ignoring the fact that something is being turned *to* in its

place."[3] Something will fill the vacuum left by the exodus of religion. As Ernest Junger said: "Deserted altars are inhabited by demons."[4]

The mixing of religion and politics is unavoidable. To prohibit one religion only opens the door for the entrance of another religion. There is no neutrality.

The Challenge of Pluralism

One of the newest challenges to the Christian worldview as it relates to politics is "pluralism." In theory, pluralism espouses an egalitarian religious and ethical theory based on the belief that personal dogmatic beliefs have no place in the social and political realms. "Pluralism is the

---

"Under pluralism all religious and nonreligious views are considered equal in establishing social and political norms. There can be no sure word from God."

---

cultural belief that there are many right ways to live and believe. There are no absolutes, so there's nothing to be dogmatic about. Find whatever works for you. If it's Jesus and Christianity, great. If it's Hinduism, that's great, too. Islam, Shintoism, Judaism . . . whatever. . . . Pluralism reduces convictions to convenient opinions and makes dogmatism an outdated approach to life and experience."[5]

Some advocates of pluralism recognize that religious values have a role to play both socially and politically, just like religion has a role to play in every aspect of life. But Christianity cannot be the *only* standard. Under pluralism all religious and nonreligious views are considered equal in establishing social and political norms. There can be no sure word from God. "Unfortunately, Christians who have been seduced by pluralism no longer say, 'Thus saith the Lord . . . ' or, 'The Bible says . . . .'

Instead, we say, 'It seems to me . . . ' or, 'It's not for me, but I'm glad it works for you.' Yet the psalmist claims that the laws of God are *right* (Psalm 19:8). Scripture is clear that there is a right and wrong and that we will personally be held accountable."[6]

Pluralism seems attractive because it eliminates the need to battle over religious first principles. The hope is to find common ethical principles that all people can agree on. Such a procedure sounds good until the theory is actually put into practice.

Let's look at a few examples. The Bible is against polygamy. In the past, the courts have agreed that it is necessary for the state to enforce the biblical requirement of monogamy over against bigamy (two wives) and polygamy (many wives): "It is contrary to the spirit of Christianity and of the civilization which Christianity has produced in the Western world."[7] In another case, the courts declared that "Bigamy and polygamy are crimes by the laws of all civilized and Christian countries. . . . To call their advocacy a tenet of religion is to offend the common sense of mankind."[8] Pluralism, if consistent, changes the way laws are made. Without any sure foundation for making laws, anything goes:

> Under the doctrine of pure pluralism—to which many secularists say they subscribe—all lifestyles are permitted. Thus, in the end, cannibalism, human sacrifice, group suicide, the Manson Family, polygamy, and kiddie porn would have to be allowed. "Who are we to say what is right and what is wrong?" is the common refrain. Clearly, society cannot long survive if this principle is pushed to its logical conclusion and everyone is free to write his own laws. Thus, we subscribe to pluralism within certain limits. We allow a wide range of behavior, even though we don't always approve of it. But we do not permit all behavior. We do not even allow all so-called "victimless" behavior— such as prostitution, drug addiction, drunkenness, and the like. The reason we don't is that our laws presuppose certain truths. Pure freedom of conscience, then, can never really be tolerated. Government neutrality on matters of religion and morals is a modern myth. We can never escape the question: Whose faith, whose values, whose God undergirds the civil laws of a nation?[9]

If it can be shown that the prohibition of polygamy is primarily religious, then under pluralism, a case could be made for allowing the practice *because* it has a religious foundation. This has already been done for homosexuality. There has been an almost universal prohibition of homosexuality, condemned by both church and state for thousands of years. "When the first great book on the English Legal system was written—Blackstone's *Commentaries on the Laws of England*—its author re-

---

"If there is no God, there is no law. How can a judge render a just decision if there is no fixed standard of justice?"

---

ferred to sodomy as 'the infamous crime against nature, committed either with man or beast . . . the very mention of which is a disgrace to human nature.'"[10]

As in England and the rest of Europe, sodomy was illegal in the thirteen American colonies. Nothing changed with the drafting of the Constitution in 1787. No supposed "right to privacy" was put in the Constitution that legalized the practice. These early Christians saw little problem in mixing religion with politics. Today, nearly half the states have legalized sodomy.

For a time, pluralism makes all opinions equal. An anti-sodomy position is just as legitimate as a pro-sodomy position; therefore, it would be illegitimate to impose an anti-sodomy position on those who want to practice sodomy. Same-sex marriages and unmarried couples would receive the same rights as legally married couples under the doctrine of pluralism. This is the policy at Stanford University. These couples have access as "domestic partners" to campus housing and university services.[11] If there is no fixed standard based on the absolutes of the Bible, then such a position is reasonable.

This same type of logic extends to the abortion issue. For example, those doctors who protect the unborn and work to save the prematurely born through heroic measures and advanced technology are no more ethical and deserving of praise than doctors who perform abortions or who deliberately snuff out the lives of the terminally ill. A consistent pluralism doctrine means that any reference to religion as a basis for an action is nullified.

Pluralism denies the Bible's view that "righteousness exalts a nation" (Proverbs 14:34), since righteousness cannot be defined in terms of any single religion or based on the collective religious will. The Bible could never be applied to political issues under the pluralism doctrine. If it was determined, for example, that a Christian judge based his ruling against abortion on his understanding of the Bible, he would most likely be overruled by a higher court. Am I exaggerating?

> U.S. District Court Judge Charles A. Moye removed the sentence of death Feb. 16 [1989] from Brandon Jones, who was convicted in 1979 of murder. Judge Moye ruled that the jury "had a duty to apply the law of the state of Georgia . . . not its own interpretation of the precepts of the Bible." The jury asked for the Bible during its consideration of a penalty for the crime, not while assessing guilt.[12]

The man was convicted of murder. The Bible says that murder is wrong. What if the people were using their understanding of the Bible when they came to the decision that he was guilty of murder based on their beliefs about the Bible? Would the judge have set Brandon Jones free if he had learned that the jury used the Bible to convict Jones?

Three additional examples might help to dispel the perceived advantages of pluralism. Under pluralism, in principle, all religions would be equal. It follows that the precepts espoused by each religion would also be equal. In the eyes of the state, there would be no fundamental difference between churches that worship God and those that worship Satan. Is this possible in a country that has been described by the Supreme Court in 1892 as a Christian nation?[13] Rhode Island, where religious pluralism got its start, sanctioned Our Lady of the Roses Wiccan Church by granting it tax-exempt status. This "church" is a coven of witches and satanists![14]

Florida no longer requires notaries to affirm "so help me God" on their written oath of office. Presidents since George Washington have taken their oath of office with a hand on an open Bible. Washington's Bible was opened to two pictures illustrating Genesis 49:13–15 on the left page and the text of Genesis 49:13–50:8 on the right. Ronald

Reagan took the oath of office on the King James Bible used by his mother, Nellie Reagan, opened to 2 Chronicles 7:14.[15] Presidents end their oath with "so help me God." The Rev. Gerard LaCerra, chancellor of the Archdiocese of Miami, understands the implications of an action that removes "so help me God" from the oath of office: "What are we supposed to base our commitments on if something like this is removed? The state?"[16] In time, pluralism leads to the messianic state which establishes its own brand of religion.

The ACLU sued a North Carolina judge because he started each court session with prayer, a brief plea to God for justice. These are the offending words:

> O Lord, our God, our Father in Heaven, we pray this morning that you will place your divine guiding hand on this courtroom and that with your mighty outstretched arm you will protect the innocent, give justice to those who have been harmed, and mercy to us all. Let truth be heard and wisdom be reflected in the light of your presence here with us today. Amen.

A United States District Judge ruled that the judge's "prayer in the courtroom is contrary to the law of the land."[17] Based on historical evidence, this would be impossible to prove.[18]

If there is no God, there is no law. How can a judge render a just decision if there is no fixed standard of justice? Why should a witness tell the truth?[19] Since the courts have consistently voted to uphold Darwinian evolutionism, how can there ever be an ethical absolute?

The Messianic State

Those Christians who believe that pluralism is the answer have not made a sincere effort to study its implications. History is filled with examples of the state assuming the role of God once all religions are made equal. If all religions are equal and religion and politics cannot mix, then how does the state justify and legitimize its existence? The state must find a way to legitimize its authority to rule, or it will be constantly overthrown by the people. When the civil magistrate and the people reject the view that the ruler's authority comes from God

(Romans 13:1)—thus making him responsible to rule in terms of God's law and making the citizenry responsible to obey as well—he makes himself a god and establishes his own laws. Thus, to oppose the king is to oppose God or the gods.

In ancient Greece, the Athenian citizen, "while free to worship his private gods, was under a duty to participate in the worship of Zeus and Apollo in the legally prescribed manner. Neglect to do so disqualified one from holding the office of magistrate."[20] This is the doctrine of pluralism in action: the citizenry can hold to a private religion while the state governs in terms of a deity of its own design. In time, even private religious beliefs and practices are no longer tolerated.

Pre-Christian Rome had a similar system. Augustus revived the older deities to solidify his position and authority as emperor. The motivation was political. "In short, it was but another illustration of the use of religion as an engine to further state policy."[21] Augustus went further than his predecessors by "setting his great uncle Julius Caesar among the gods, and commanded that the worship of the Divine Julius should not be less than the worship of Apollo, Jupiter, and the other gods. Augustus thus initiated what has been called the real religion of pre-Christian Rome—the worship of the head of the state. At his death Augustus too joined the ranks of the gods, as did other emperors after him."[22] Like Greece, Rome tolerated private religious belief and practice "as long as they did not intervene in the political arena, where the state religion enjoyed a monopoly."[23] In time, however, religious toleration ceased. Refusal to worship Caesar was a manifestation of disloyalty that was often met with cruel retribution, although refusal to worship Jupiter was still tolerated. The emperor was a god who was a cut above the traditional gods, Jupiter included.

With the entrance of Judaism and Christianity on the Roman social and political scene with their declaration of the *shema*—"Hear, O Israel! The LORD is our God, the LORD is one!" (Deuteronomy 6:4; Mark 12:29)—an immediate conflict arose. In time, just to be a Christian was an offense against Rome and the gods, especially the emperor who, during the reign of Domitian (81–96), was addressed "as *dominus et deus*, 'my Lord and God.'"[24] The Christians could avoid persecution, but at great cost. "Any accused person who denied Christ and gave satisfactory proof that he abjured his errors, by adoring the gods and the emperor's image and cursing Christ, was to be immediately acquitted."[25] So much for the benefits of pluralism.

Rome Revisited

You would be wrong if you thought that the deification of the state is solely an attribute of the ancient world. The French Revolution of the eighteenth century resurrected the notion of the deification of the state. While the Christian religion would no longer be mixed with French politics, this did not mean that religion itself would be banished. The vacuum was filled with a new god. The French "proclaimed the goddess of Reason in Notre-Dame Cathedral in Paris and in other churches in France. . . . In Paris, the goddess was personified by an actress, Demoiselle Candeille, carried shoulder-high into the cathedral by men dressed in Roman costumes."[26] With the expulsion of the old religion of Christianity went the significance of that religion. The French were so opposed to mixing the Christian religion with politics or anything else, that they overturned the entire social order by reconfiguring the calendar:

> It is noteworthy that the two greatest atheistic regimes in history—the revolutionary governments of France in 1792 and Russia in 1929— tried to change the traditional week, hoping thereby to destroy Christianity. The French set up a ten-day week and the Soviets a five-day week, and both were rigidly enforced, but each lasted only a few years.[27]

Even the traditional way of dating is beginning to change among intellectuals and liberal theologians. The symbols B.C. and A.D.—"before Christ" and *anno Domini* (year of our Lord)—are being rejected in favor of B.C.E. and C.E. ("before the common era" and "common era").

The French Revolution consolidated power into a new nationalism that enticed some "to speak of the 'goddess France.' It meant that those who fought for France were no longer simply doing a job for which they were paid, but were patriots rendering due obeisance to a deity. For them, to do their duty was to do their *sacred* duty, language that has

remained part of the liturgy of patriotism to the present, even in offic-
ially atheistic countries like the Soviet Union."[28]

The March of God on Earth

The once-popular and influential philosopher G. W. F. Hegel described
the state as "the march of God through the world." Hegel proposed that
the state should be worshipped because the state is "the manifestation
of the Divine on earth."[29] One would be hard pressed to find modern
political pundits who use Hegel's blunt language, but more often than
not actions speak louder than words. For modern statists the political

---

**"Some religion, even if it is atheism
or paganism, will always be mixed
with politics. To exclude Christianity
only opens the door to other religions."**

---

sphere is no less divine than the city-states of Greece and Rome and
the deified nationalism of France, Stalinist Russia, and Nazi Germany.
For many modern-day politicians the state is a saving institution instead
of a gift from God to protect us against violence. The state plays the
role of benefactor instead of its biblical role as judge. "The idol state
uses the language of compassion because its intention is a messianic
one. It finds the masses harassed and helpless, like sheep without a
shepherd, needing a savior."[30] The state promises to set up heaven on
earth through coercion and the consolidation of power in the hands of
a few. The result is a loss of freedom for the many. It does this in the
name of its religion.

> Now [Herod] was very angry with the people of Tyre and Sidon; and
> with one accord they came to him, and having won over Blastus the
> king's chamberlain, they were asking for peace, *because their country*

was fed by the king's country. And on an appointed day Herod, having put on his royal apparel, took his seat on the rostrum and began delivering an address to them. And the people kept crying out, "The voice of a god and not of a man!" And immediately an angel of the Lord struck him because he did not give God the glory, and he was eaten by worms and died. (Acts 12:20–23, emphasis added)

As this passage shows, God does not tolerate pluralism. From what we have seen, we can conclude that it is impossible to separate religion from politics. Herod fed the people and demanded worship from the people, and the people were quick to respond favorably. Some religion, even if it is atheism or paganism, will always be mixed with politics. To exclude Christianity only opens the door to other religions.

A Closer Look at the Bible

Politics derives its authority from God (Romans 13:1). While God's power is unlimited, all earthly power, politics included, is limited: "The Most High God is ruler over the realm of mankind, and . . . He sets over it whomever He wishes" (Daniel 5:21). The church reflected on these truths and began to assess its rulers in terms of biblical norms. "During the eighth and ninth centuries the Christian church effected nothing short of a revolution in the forms of Western politics. Put briefly, there developed an idea of the pervasive religious and moral responsibility of the ruler."[31] The ruler was neither divine nor exempt from heaven's rule. The Christian religion specified the ruler's duties and limitations. There was a mix of religion and politics.

As we will see, the Bible has a great deal to say about the relationship between religion and politics. Bear in mind that there is no neutrality. To separate Christianity from politics is only to align politics with any number of antireligious concepts. As Abraham Kuyper, former Prime Minister of the Netherlands, has written, "no political scheme has ever become dominant which was not founded in a specific religious or anti-religious conception."[32] In time, this antireligious fervor becomes a religion itself.

Rulers as Ministers of God

Scripture tells us that civil rulers are put in positions of authority for our good (Romans 13:4). The civil magistrate is a minister of God. The word "minister" is the same Greek word that is translated *deacon* and *servant*. There are a number of rulers today who still retain the title of "minister," reflecting the biblical language of civil responsibility. The highest civil official in Japan and England is given the title of "Prime Minister." Such a title has ethical—religious—connotations: "By me [the Personal Wisdom of God] kings reign, and rulers decree justice. By me princes rule, and nobles, all who judge rightly" (Proverbs 8:15–16). The truly just ruler will acknowledge that true justice is derived by following God's wisdom. "Both Charles the Bald, his grandson, and Alfred in England, compared themselves to Solomon, ruling in accordance with divine wisdom, and Alfred as a lawgiver saw himself in a succession of lawgivers beginning with Moses."[33]

Rulers as Ministers Under God's Dominion

Rulers are to serve God with reverence (Psalm 2:11). It is God who "will cut off the spirit of princes; He is feared by the kings of the earth" (Psalm 76:12). A time will come when all "the nations will fear the name of the LORD, and all the kings of the earth Thy glory" (Psalm 102:15). The New Testament has not nullified the role of God's authority over rulers since Jesus "is the image of the invisible God, the firstborn of all creation. For by Him all things were created, both in the heavens and on earth, visible and invisible, *whether thrones or dominions or rulers or authorities—all things have been created by Him and for Him*" (Colossians 1:15–16, emphasis added). Jesus *"has put* [past tense] *all things* [including politics] in subjection under His feet" (1 Corinthians 15:27, emphasis added). The rulers of this world were required to understand God's wisdom. Their lack of understanding led them to crucify the Lord of Glory (1 Corinthians 2:8).

Rulers as Ministers of Righteousness

The civil magistrate, as he is described in Romans 13:1–4 and 1 Peter 2:13–14, is to promote the good and punish evildoers. What standard is a ruler to use to determine what is good behavior and what is evil be-havior? God is the one who gives the ruler his legal right to hold office, establishes his legitimacy of authority to rule, and demands that he make just and righteous judgments in praising good behavior and pun-ishing evil behavior. Are we then to assume that the magistrate is free to rule without any consideration of religion? Keep in mind that we are

---

"The political realm is ministerial. It demands faith and allegiance to God as the sole Governor of the world."

---

not maintaining that rulers are to force people to become Christians or to go to church. The Bible does require, however, that rulers base their judgments on religious presuppositions. This is why Jethro instructed Moses to teach the rulers and the people the statutes and the laws, and to "make known to them the way in which they are to walk, and the work they are to do" (Exodus 18:20; Deuteronomy 17:18–20; Psalm 2:10–12; 2 Samuel 23:3–4).

Rulers Mixing Religion and Politics

Noah, an agent of the civil magistrate under the authority of God, is given authority to execute murderers (Genesis 9:6–7); Joseph is made ruler in Egypt (Genesis 41:38–49); Moses was the civil ruler in Israel and, because of Jethro's counsel, appointed lesser magistrates to perform civil duties (Exodus 18:13–27); "case laws" are listed for the govern-ment of family, church, and civil government (Exodus 21–23); God in-structs both priests and kings to follow the law of God (Deuteronomy 17:14–20); the book of Judges is filled with examples of civil rulers: Othniel (Judges 3:9), Ehud (3:15), Shamgar (3:31), Deborah/Barak (4:4, 6), Gideon (6:11), Jephthah (11:1), and Samson (13:24). God called upon them to deliver the nation from political oppression brought on by sin, every man doing what was right in his own eyes (Judges 17:6). The writer to the Hebrew Christians commends these civil rulers:

> And what more shall I say? For time will fail me if I tell of Gideon, Barak, Samson, Jephthah, of David and Samuel and the prophets, *who by faith conquered kingdoms, [and] performed acts of righteousness*. . . . (Hebrews 11:32–33, emphasis added)

Their deeds were acts of faith. The political realm is ministerial. It demands faith and allegiance to God as the sole Governor of the world (Isaiah 9:6–7).

The books of Samuel, Kings, and Chronicles tell of the rise and fall of kings and kingdoms, with individual kings singled out for their faithfulness (2 Chronicles 25:1–2; 26:3–4; 27:1–2). Daniel served as one of Darius's three commissioners (Daniel 6). Nehemiah was appointed governor in Israel (Nehemiah 5:14).

The New Testament is not without examples of political involvement, although to a lesser extent. Keep in mind that Israel was a captive nation at the time of Jesus' incarnation and ministry. The civil rulers of Israel (elders of the people) could not even implement their own law in their own country (John 18:31), but not because of any theological restriction set forth in Scripture. Given the opportunity, the Jewish state would have been fully operative.

John the Baptist did not tell the Roman soldiers to abandon their positions within the state. Jesus and the Apostle Paul had the utmost respect for civil rulers. In fact, Jesus spoke more harshly against the religious leaders of His day, and only used one derogatory remark against a civil official, calling Herod "that fox," probably having reference to his being controlled by a woman (Luke 13:32). Paul commended the city treasurer Erastus (Romans 16:23). Prayers are to "be made on behalf of all men, for kings and all who are in authority. . . ." (1 Timothy 2:1–2).

> That God is vitally concerned with political affairs is quite easy to demonstrate: it is God who ordained governments in the first place (Rom. 13:1; Rom. 2:21). He is the One who establishes particular kings (Prov. 16:12; Psa. 119:46, 47; 82:1, 2). Therefore, He commands our obedience to rulers (Rom. 13:1–3). Rulers are commanded to rule

on His terms (Psa. 2:10ff.). Even in the New Testament activity of political import is discoverable. Jesus urged payment of taxes to *de facto* governments (Matt. 22:15–22). In response to reminders of King Herod's political threats against Him, Jesus publicly rebuked the king by calling him a vixen (Luke 13:32). He taught that a judge is unjust if he does not fear God (Luke 18:2, 6). John the Baptist openly criticized King Herod (Luke 3:19, 20). Peter refused to obey authorities who commanded him to cease preaching (Acts 5:29). The Apostle John referred to the Roman Empire as "the beast" (Rev. 13).[34]

Politics, then, is people acting and making decisions about civil relationships based upon a set of first principles that have a religious foundation. To deny that this area of decision-making is to be affected by religion is to deny the lordship of Jesus Christ over a particular area of life.

10

"THE CHRISTIAN'S CITIZENSHIP IS IN HEAVEN"

In the modern world, then, each Christian is a citizen of two nations: An earthly nation like France, England, or the U.S.A., and the heavenly nation (Ephesians 2:6; not of this world, John 18:36), the church. Though we belong entirely to Christ, we do not on that account renounce our citizenship in the earthly nations, any more than we leave our earthly families. Indeed, we seek to be good citizens, for those earthly nations themselves, and their rulers, received their authority from God (Romans 13:1–7).

JOHN M. FRAME

I will protect the German people,' Hitler shouted. 'You take care of the church. You pastors should worry about getting people to heaven and leave this world to me.' "[1] Adolf Hitler's angry response was directed at Martin Niemöller, a decorated submarine commander in the First World War, an ardent nationalist, and a minister of the gospel. Niemöller had written *From U-Boat to Pulpit* in 1933, showing that "the fourteen years of the [Weimar] Republic had been 'years of darkness.'" In a final word inserted at the end of the book, he added that Hitler's triumph at last brought light to Germany.[2] He soon learned that the light was an incendiary bomb that would destroy the hopes and freedoms of the German people. That light would also be used to ignite gas ovens in the extermination of millions of Jews and other "undesirables." By 1935, "Niemöller had become completely disillusioned."[3]

Niemöller became an ardent critic of Hitler and his policies, "protesting against the anti-Christian tendencies of the regime, denouncing the government's anti-Semitism and demanding an end to the state's interference in the churches."[4] Not everyone followed Niemöller's lead. Numerous pastors swore a personal oath of allegiance and obedience to Adolf Hitler. Other pastors were sent to concentration camps for their defiance. Niemöller was imprisoned for his efforts.

Why did many in the church comply with Hitler and his policies? Why did they act, as Hitler described them, like "submissive dogs . . . that sweat with embarrassment when you talk to them"?[5] For the most part, the people believed that their heavenly citizenship obligated them blindly to accept the prevailing civil requirements of citizenship and to remain silent no matter what atrocities might be committed. "In no country with the exception of Czarist Russia did the clergy become by tradition so completely servile to the political authority of the State."[6]

Christian faith that adheres to an exclusively heavenly citizenship has no effect on the Christian's civil citizenship since he is simply a pilgrim and a stranger on his way to heaven. Hitler took advantage of this belief. Niemöller taught otherwise: "We have no more thought of using our own powers to escape the arm of the authorities than had the Apostles of old. No more are we ready to keep silent at man's behest when God commands us to speak. For it is, and must remain, the case that we must obey God rather than man."[7] A Christian's heavenly citizenship, Niemöller concluded, must have an impact in the world in which he lives.

Dual Citizenship

Supposedly, the Christian's heavenly citizenship automatically nullifies any earthly citizenship. But the Apostle Paul saw no contradiction in claiming his Roman citizenship (Acts 16:37–39; 22:22–29) and maintaining that he was also a citizen of heaven (Philippians 3:20). There is no contradiction in Peter's command to us to submit ourselves "to every human institution, whether to a king as the one in authority, or to governors as sent by him for the punishment of evildoers and the praise

---

"Christian faith that adheres to an exclusively heavenly citizenship has no effect on the Christian's civil citizenship . . . Hitler took advantage of this belief."

---

of those who do right" (1 Peter 2:13–14) and his words to the officers of the temple when he and the apostles said, "We must obey God rather than men" (Acts 5:29).

The Christian is a citizen of a number of locales—a city, county, state, and nation. For example, the Apostle Paul was a Roman citizen (Acts 22:27–29) of the city of Tarsus in the region of Cilicia (21:39) and a resident of Jerusalem in the district of Judea (22:3). Had Israel not been subject to the sovereignty of Rome, Paul could have exercised his tribal citizenship as a resident of the tribe of Benjamin (Philippians 3:5). Paul had multiple civil citizenships. The concept of a single citizenship has more in common with pagan Greece than with biblical Christianity:

> No one could become a citizen at Athens if he was a citizen in another city; for it was a religious impossibility to be at the same time a member of two cities, as it also was to be a member of two families.[8]

In the United States an individual has a national, state, county, and city citizenship. In some states borough governments (e.g., Pennsylvania, New Jersey, New York, Minnesota) operate, and in others parish governments (e.g., Louisiana) operate. Each of the many civil authorities holds real but delegated power and sovereignty in these locales.

Their real authority and sovereignty can be used to curtail the power of another legitimate government that might abuse its authority, or an illegitimate governing power assuming rule through coercion.

Through multiple civil citizenships citizens have access to the seats of power where influence can be exerted on a local level. Abolition of these many civil distinctions leads to despotism and tyranny. Adolph Hitler was able to consolidate his power by eliminating the many civil distinctions within the nation:

> He had abolished the separate powers of the historic states and made them subject to the central authority of the Reich, which was in his hands. . . . "Popular assemblies" of the states were abolished, the sovereign powers of the states were transferred to the Reich, all state governments were placed under the Reich government and the state governors put under the administration of the Reich Minister of the Interior.[9]

One of the tenets of Marxism is the "gradual abolition of the distinction between town and country, by a more equable distribution of the population over the country."[10] With the abolition of the distinction went reduction of sovereignty with all power going to a central government. Our American constitutional founders, on the other hand, designed a limited civil government which decentralized power and authority. Our forefathers feared the type of government that gave birth to Nazism and Communism.

Ultimately, the Christian is a citizen of God's kingdom. In Philippians 3:20, Paul mentions this aspect of citizenship: "For our citizenship is in heaven, from which also we eagerly wait for a Savior, the Lord Jesus Christ." This idea corresponds to Jesus informing Nicodemus that he must be "born again" (literally, born from above) (John 3:3; John 14:1-3). In effect, he must become a citizen of heaven. An individual's Christian citizenship does not cancel his earthly citizenship and corresponding civil obligations, however.

In another sense, the Christian's heavenly citizenship makes him an alien, stranger, and exile on earth (Hebrews 11:13; 1 Peter 2:11). The Christian does not repudiate his earthly citizenship while acting as a pilgrim. But his earthly citizenship is not to be considered primary. Earthly citizenship is temporary and has meaning only within the context of a biblical moral order—the kingdom of God that encompasses all citizenship. The Christian is told to "seek first His kingdom and His righteousness. . . ." (Matthew 6:33).

The Christian has an obligation to follow the law of God as it applies to all locales. God's law is the standard for all citizenships. Our heavenly citizenship involves comprehensive lawkeeping. Jesus said, "If you love Me, you will keep My commandments" (John 14:15). Jesus

---

"When Scripture speaks about obeying the civil magistrate, . . . citizens must obey. When state laws conflict with the laws of heaven, the Christian's first obligation is to his heavenly citizenship."

---

does not restrict the locale of lawkeeping; therefore, we can conclude that the keeping of His commandments includes every type of citizenship without exception.

When Scripture speaks about obeying the civil magistrate (Romans 13:1-7; 1 Peter 2:13-17), citizens must obey. When state laws conflict with the laws of heaven, the Christian's first obligation is to his heavenly citizenship (Acts 5:29). While the Christian lives on earth, he remains responsible to various ecclesiastical and civil governments, but he looks for the day when his heavenly citizenship will be fully realized:

> All these [Old Testament believers] died in faith, without receiving the promises, but having seen them and having welcomed them from a distance, and having confessed that they were strangers and exiles on the earth. . . . But as it is, they desire a better country, that is a heavenly one. (Hebrews 11:13, 16; 1 Peter 2:11)

The church is spoken of as a citizenship: "So then you are no longer strangers and aliens, but you are fellow-citizens with the saints, and are of God's household" (Ephesians 2:19).

Paul's Example

The Apostle Paul saw no inconsistency in taking advantage of his Roman citizenship (Acts 16:37–39; 22:22–29) while maintaining that he was also a citizen of heaven (Philippians 3:20). Paul did not deny his Roman citizenship and claim heavenly citizenship when he was taken to be "examined by scourging" (Acts 22:24, 25, 28). "And when they stretched him out with thongs, Paul said to the centurion who was standing by, 'Is it lawful for you to scourge a man who is a Roman and uncondemned?'" (22:25). Why didn't Paul just "take it," content in the fact that he was a citizen of heaven? Instead, he used the privileges of Roman citizenship to his advantage. While some had purchased their citizenship with large sums of money, Paul "was actually born a citizen" (22:28).

Nowhere do we find Paul repudiating the privileges that came with being a Roman citizen. We should keep in mind that the Caesars considered themselves to be gods. To be actively involved in the realm of politics does not mean that politics has to be free of all pagan thought. Paul proclaimed an unadulterated message to these pagan rulers hoping to persuade them of their religious folly. After hearing Paul's defense of the gospel, King Agrippa replied to him, "In a short time you will persuade me to become a Christian" (Acts 26:28).

On many occasions the apostle used all of the privileges of Roman citizenship to his advantage by appealing, not to heaven before the Romans (certainly Paul did appeal to heaven, since he tells us to "pray without ceasing" [1 Thessalonians 5:17]) but to Caesar, the seat of Roman civil authority (Acts 25:11). Of course, he was using Caesar as a way to advance the gospel to bring others into heavenly citizenship.

The Sovereignty of Satan

Related to the citizenship issue is the status of Satan in the world. If Satan is sovereign over this world, then it stands to reason that Christians, whose citizenship is elsewhere, cannot participate in a world controlled by the devil. Paul, however, had no trouble dealing with pagan emperors who thought of themselves as gods, as we have seen above.

Some Christians will go so far as to declare that secular government is "the province of the sovereignty of Satan."[11] This belief is based, in part, on the temptation narratives of Matthew and Luke where Satan offers the king-

---

> ## "If Satan possessed all the kingdoms of the earth prior to the Crucifixion (a debatable point), he certainly doesn't have them now."

---

doms of the world to Jesus. Satan, showing Jesus "all the kingdoms of the world, and their glory," promises: "All these things will I give You, if you fall down and worship me" (Matthew 4:9), "for it has been handed over to me, and I give it to whomever I wish" (Luke 4:6). According to this theory, Satan is in control of political power structures.

Robert Duncan Culver, a supporter of this thesis, writes:

> It is noteworthy that Jesus did not dispute the claim of dominion over the kingdoms of the world (*kosmos*). His answer was an implicit acknowledgment of the legitimacy of Satan's claim. Under the providence of God it is his to give, or else there was no temptation. In such a case Jesus might have laughed at Satan rather than to have answered with sober quotations of relevant Scripture.[12]

There are several problems with this interpretation. First, we know that Satan is a liar (Genesis 3:4–5). Jesus calls him "a liar, and the father of lies" (John 8:44). Second, does the truth have to be told before a temptation can be real? Let's suppose a politician is offered a million dollars if he votes a certain way on some upcoming legislation. The politician agrees and takes the money. As soon as he does, an FBI agent appears, reads him his rights, and then arrests him for accepting a bribe. The money is taken from the politician and put back in the custody of the Justice Department that set up the sting operation. The man who offered him the money did not own the money. In fact, the entire operation was a lie. The crime was in the willingness to accept the bribe to influence legislation.

Third, Jesus' "sin" (if I dare use the word) would have been to accept Satan's offer whether it was legitimate or not. Once He did that, the sin would have been committed whether Satan had possession of anything or not. Satan then could have laughed in derision after informing Jesus that the kingdoms were not his anyway. The damage, however, would have been done.

Finally, we know that after the death and resurrection of Jesus, Satan's authority is severely limited: "Now judgment is upon this world; now the ruler of this world shall be cast out" (John 12:31). Satan's status in the world has changed significantly. Jesus is the "King of kings and Lord of lords" (Revelation 19:16). If Satan possessed all the kingdoms of the earth prior to the Crucifixion (a debatable point), he certainly doesn't have them now.

Are the Powers Evil?

Some go even further in their evaluation of political power by claiming that power is evil in and of itself, especially when it is institutionalized in the realm of politics. The claim is made that Christians cannot get involved in politics because the very nature of government is satanic. Supposedly, Jesus made this very clear in John 19:11 when He stated that Pilate's power was given to him "from above," that is, from rebellious angels. Jacques Ellul in *The Subversion of Christianity* maintains that "'from above' does not denote either God or the emperor but the *exousia* of political power, which is a rebel *exousia*, an angel in revolt against God."[13] Is this possible? Jesus tells Nicodemus that he must be born "from above" (John 3:3). The same Greek word is used in both places. Paul tells us that the authorities "which exist are established by God" (Romans 13:1). The institution of civil government is God-ordained. This does not mean that those in power acknowledge God's sovereignty over them (Daniel 4). Neither does it mean that Christians should not get involved in the political process. Not to be involved in some capacity is to deny God as the One who establishes the powers that be.

Christians would agree that the abuse of power is evil, as is the abuse of wealth, sex, and freedom. But is power evil in and of itself? While it is true that God has chosen the weak things of the world to confound the strong, it is equally true that God has invested authority and power in governmental institutions like family, church, and civil government.

It is the *love* of money that is the root of all kinds of evil, not money itself. Money is God's good gift to man. God created the land of Havilah with gold, and Scripture tells us that "the gold of that land is good" (Genesis 2:12). But money, like power, can be abused. Men in positions of authority often abuse power. Nebuchadnezzar, king of Babylon, is a perfect example of the legitimacy and the abuse of power. God judged the king for his claim of absolute and autonomous sovereignty and power:

> The king reflected and said, "Is this not Babylon the great, which I myself have built as a royal residence by the might of my power and for the glory of my majesty?" While the word was in the king's mouth, a voice came from heaven saying, "King Nebuchadnezzar, to you it is declared: sovereignty has been removed from you, and you will be driven away from mankind, and your dwelling place will be with the beasts of the field." (Daniel 4:30–32a)

In time, however, God restored the king's sovereignty, and "surpassing greatness was added" to him (4:36). How could God restore the king if these powers are evil? Here also is an answer to the assertion that Satan possessed "all the kingdoms of the world" and offered them to Jesus. How could God remove and restore sovereignty when Satan possessed it?

The Present Status of the Devil

Like all creatures, the devil has certain limitations. Even under the Old Covenant, Satan had to be granted permission by God before he could act (Job 1:6–12; 2:1–7). Satan's limitations have been multiplied since the crucifixion, resurrection, and ascension of Jesus.

The Bible shows us that if we "resist the devil he will flee from" us (James 4:7). The only power that Satan has over the Christian is the power we give him and the power granted to him by God (2 Corinthians 12:7–12). Scripture tells us that Satan is defeated, disarmed, and spoiled (Colossians 2:15; Revelation 12:7–8; Mark 3:27). He has fallen (Luke 10:18) and was thrown down (Revelation 12:9). He was crushed under the feet of the early Christians, and by implication, under the feet of all Christians throughout the ages (Romans 16:20). He has lost authority over Christians (Colossians 1:13). He has been judged (John 16:11). He cannot touch a Christian (1 John 5:18). His works have been destroyed (1 John 3:8). He has nothing (John 14:30). He must flee when resisted (James 4:7). He is bound (Mark 3:27; Luke 11:20). Finally, the gates of hell shall not overpower the advancing church of the Lord Jesus Christ (Matthew 16:18). Surely Satan is alive, but he is not well on planet Earth.

Satan as the "God of this World"

So then, what does Paul mean when he describes Satan as the "god of this world"[14] or of this age? (2 Corinthians 4:4). Supposedly this verse teaches that Satan has all power and authority in this dispensation and in the locale of planet Earth: God is the God of heaven and of the age to come, and Satan is the god of Earth and this present evil age. This dualistic view of the universe may be part of Greek pagan philosophy, but it has no place in biblical theology.

While it's true that the devil is said to be the god of this age, we know that God is "the King of the ages" (1 Timothy 1:17). Jesus is in possession of "all authority," in both *heaven* and *earth* (Matthew 28:18–20):

> The modern Dispensationalist goes so far as to say that Satan is in control of this present world. He overlooks the obvious fact that the only three passages of Scripture which denominate Satan "the prince of this world" assert that Christ by His death defeated Satan as prince of the world. With a view to His impending death Jesus said: "Now shall the prince of this world be cast out" [John 12:31]; "the prince of this world cometh, and he hath nothing in me" [John 14:30]; "the prince of this world is judged" [John 16:11].[15]

In addition, we know that Satan's power has not increased since Job's day. He must still seek permission to tempt God's people (Job 1:6–12; Luke 22:31). This is especially true under the new and better covenant inaugurated by Jesus Christ. Gods do not have to ask permission. As the above verses make clear, Satan is a second-class creature who has been cast out and judged: "The ruler of this world *shall be* cast out" (John 12:31, emphasis added); "the ruler of this world *has been* judged" (John 16:11, emphasis added).

What, then, does the apostle mean when he describes Satan as "the god of this age"? First, we must never allow one passage to finalize our understanding of a particular doctrine. Scripture must be compared with Scripture. There are no contradictions. Therefore, we can't have God as "the King of the ages" and Satan as "the god of this age." We can't say that Satan has been judged and cast out and still maintain that he is the god of this world similar to the way Jehovah is God of this world.

What theological point is Paul trying to make? Jesus tells the Pharisees that the devil is their father (John 8:44). We know that Satan is not their biological father. Rather, he is their spiritual father in that they rejected their true Father and His Son, Jesus Christ:

> Physically these Jews, to be sure, are children of Abraham; but spiritually and morally—and *that* was the issue—they are the children of the devil.[16]

Jesus is describing the devil as one who gives birth to a worldview that includes lying and murder. In this sense, Satan is their spiritual father. In the same way, Satan is a god to those who cling to the fading glory of Moses, "the ministry of death" (2 Corinthians 3:7). This is the age over which he is a god, an age that "has no glory on account of the glory that surpasses it" (3:10). That glory is the finished work of Jesus Christ that has surpassed the administration of the blood of bulls and goats. The unbelieving Jews of Jesus' day were still clinging to the temple and the sacrifices when the true Lamb of God who had come to take away the sins of the world had been in their midst (John 1:29). They had crucified God's Lamb who was in fact the "Lord of Glory" (1 Corinthians 2:8).

Second, the devil is chosen as a god by "those who are perishing," and he must blind them before they will follow him: "The god of this world *has blinded the minds of the unbelieving*, that they *might not see the light of the gospel* of the glory of Christ, who is the image of God" (2 Corinthians 4:4, emphasis added). This passage teaches that unbelievers are *fooled* into believing that the Old Covenant where the "veil remains unlifted" is the way to life (3:14). Satan is the god of the "ministry of death." The god of this age keeps them in bondage, "but whenever a man turns to the Lord, the veil is taken away" (3:16), and he no longer perceives Satan as god. Freedom from the ministry of death only comes where the Spirit of the Lord is: "Now the Lord is the Spirit; and where the Spirit of the Lord is, there is liberty" (3:17). But Satan has blinded the eyes of the unbelieving so they cannot see the lifted veil. They are still trusting in the Old Covenant. Satan is their god of choice.

Third, like idols in general, the devil is by nature not a god (Galatians 4:8; Deuteronomy 32:17; Psalm 96:5; Isaiah 44:9–20; 1 Corinthians 8:4; 10:20). In Philippians 3:18–19, Paul tells us that those who are "enemies of the cross of Christ" worship their appetite: "For many walk, of whom I often told you, and now tell you even weeping, that they are enemies of the cross of Christ, whose end is destruction, *whose god is their appetite*, and whose glory is in their shame, *who set their minds on earthly things* (emphasis added)." The appetite is not a god, but it can be chosen as a god. Satan is not a god, but he can be set up as an idol similar to the way the children of Israel set up the golden calf (Exodus 32:1–10; Isaiah 44:9–28).

Fourth, the only way Satan can pass himself off as a god is first to blind his victims. Keep in mind that Jesus described the devil as "a liar, and the father of lies" (John 8:44). Though Satan masquerades as a god, this does not make him a god.

Satan wishes, albeit vainly, to set himself up as God, and sinners, in rebelling against the true God, subject themselves to him who is the author of their rebellion. The unregenerate serve Satan as though he were their God. They do not thereby, however, escape from the dominion of the one true God. On the contrary, they bring themselves under His righteous judgment; for Satan is a creature and not a God to be served (cf. Romans 1:18, 25). Just as there is one in the world and every pretended alternative to it is a false no-gospel, so there is only one God of the universe and every other "deity" whom men worship and serve is a false no-god.[17]

When all the evidence is in, we learn that Satan is the god of an age that was passing away. He is the god of choice for those who reject the finished redemptive work of Jesus Christ. This age and this world

---

"When the church *makes* Satan the god of this age, it has fallen for one of the devil's schemes—giving him a lot more credit and power than he deserves or possesses."

---

are used "in an *ethical* sense, [denoting] the *immoral realm of disobedience* rather than the all-inclusive, extensive scope of creation, [representing] the life of man apart from God and bound to sinful impulses, [a world] ethically separated from God."[18] Martin Luther put it well:

> And though this world, with devils filled,
> Should threaten to undo us,
> We will not fear, for God hath willed
> His truth to triumph through us.
> The prince of darkness grim
> We tremble not for him;
> His rage we can endure,
> For lo! his doom is sure,
> One little word shall fell him.[19]

Calling Satan the god of this age is more a reflection on the condition of this age than the real status of the devil. Chrysostom comments that "Scripture frequently uses the term *god*, not in regard of the dignity that is so designated, but of the weakness of those in subjection to it; as when he calls mammon lord and belly god: but the belly is neither therefore God nor mammon Lord, save only of those who bow themselves to them."[20]

When the church *makes* Satan the god of this age, it has fallen for one of the devil's schemes—giving him a lot more credit and power than he deserves or possesses. He is quite satisfied in having anyone believe one of his lies.

PART 4

THE CHRISTIAN AND THE KINGDOM

11

"GOD'S KINGDOM HAS NOT COME"

*The presence and power of the kingdom was
visible to all [the early church.] In spite of
bitter persecution thousands were being converted to the Christian faith. They saw
"greater works" than the physical miracles
which Jesus Himself performed. The life-
transforming evidence was before their eyes.
Sane men do not dogmatically affirm to
other sane men that there is a sun in the
heavens. The gospel which the Baptist,
Jesus, and Paul proclaimed was in the strictest sense the gospel of the kingdom which the
Prophets spoke (cf. Acts 28:23, 31).*

RODERICK CAMPBELL

To espouse the belief that God's kingdom is solely future means
that we are living in a purely secular kingdom with purely secular
laws cut off from the governance of heaven. This is the worldview of
deism! If this is the view of any part of the church, then the secularists
are right in condemning the mixing of any of God's laws with those of
the state. How can God as a *future* King have any say in the affairs of a
present kingdom under the rule of another king? This would be like a

future presidential candidate telling the current president how to run his affairs. A future president has no legal standing to make such a demand.

The Kingdom Has Come

If the kingdom is defined in political terms, so that Jesus personally and physically rules from Jerusalem in the midst of a rebuilt temple, a renewed sacrificial system, and the reestablishment of the Old Testament theocratic government, then God's kingdom has not yet come.[1] On the other hand, if the kingdom is defined as a spiritual manifestation of the work of Christ in this world, a work that is the transforming and regenerating work of the Holy Spirit in the lives of sinners, with Jesus enthroned at His Father's right hand, where presently He rules as "King of kings and Lord of lords" (Revelation 19:16), then it can be said that the kingdom has come.

An objection often arises, however. Some maintain that only the kingdom fully realized attests to its inauguration. But does an inauguration of something have to be mature before it is that thing? For example, a tree that is four feet tall is still a tree. It will always be called a tree until it ceases to exist. A business that starts this year with only two employees may not realize a profit for three years, but it remains a business until it goes out of business. Fledgling as such operations may be at the beginning, it is still a business along with such conglomerates as IBM and General Motors.

"A Nation Producing the Fruit of It"

Before we move into a study of the details of the view that the kingdom has come, it might be profitable to consider an important passage of Scripture that can shed light on the subject of the present reality of God's kingdom. In the parable of the landowner, Jesus indicts the chief priests and Pharisees for their rejection of His messiahship. He predicts that as the Heir of the Landowner, He will be cast out of the vineyard and be killed (Matthew 21:38). Jesus relates this to the kingdom in several ways. First, Israel had the kingdom, an extension of the Old Covenant kingdom; therefore, it was a present reality: "The kingdom of God *will be taken away from you,* and be given to a nation producing the fruit of it" (21:43, emphasis added). Jesus could not take away what they did not have. Second, there is no mention of a postponement or a parenthesis. Jesus does not say, "The coming of the kingdom will be

---

"If the kingdom is defined in political terms, . . . then God's kingdom has not yet come. On the other hand, if the kingdom is defined as a spiritual manifestation of the work of Christ in this world, . . . then it can be said that the kingdom has come."

---

delayed for another time." Third, the kingdom will "be given to a nation producing the fruit of it." The "deed" to the kingdom is transferred to a new nation. Fourth, it is obvious from the apostles' question in Acts 1:6 that they believed the kingdom had been taken from Israel, because they ask, "Lord, is it at this time You are restoring the kingdom to Israel?"

Where and when is the kingdom if it was taken from the unfaithful Jews of Jesus' day? According to Matthew 21:43, it resides with "a nation producing the fruit of it." And what is that nation? "But you [Christians] are a chosen race, a royal priesthood, *a holy nation,* a people for God's own possession, that you may proclaim the excellencies of Him who has called you out of darkness into His marvelous light" (1 Peter 2:9, emphasis added). As any student of Scripture will recognize, Peter's source for these descriptions is the Old Testament (Deuteronomy 10:15; Isaiah 43:20–21; 61:6; 66:21; Exodus 19:6; Deuteronomy 7:6). These passages describe God's relationship with the *nation* of Israel. But with the coming of the Messiah, and the rejection of God's Heir by the unfaithful, the kingdom has been taken away and given to "a nation producing the fruit of it"—a reconstituted Israel, a people made up of believing Jews (Acts 2:5, 9–11, 37–42; 3:11–4:4) and Gentiles (Acts 10:34–45): "For you once were not a people, but now you are the people of God; you had not received mercy, but now you have received mercy" (1 Peter 2:10). And what follows? Peter exhorts them to produce the fruit commensurate with being a holy nation: "Beloved, I urge you as aliens and strangers to abstain from fleshly lusts, which wage war against the soul. Keep your behavior excellent among the Gentiles, so that in the thing in which they slander you as evildoers, they may on account of your good deeds, as they observe them, glorify God in the day of visitation" (1 Peter 2:11–12). When will the kingdom be restored to Israel? It was restored to the Israel of God (Galatians 6:16) soon after Pentecost.

The Need for Definitions

From a study of the Old Testament we realize that in some sense God's kingdom was a present reality even before Jesus came to earth. The New Testament does not indicate that it has somehow been interrupted or postponed for a distant future fulfillment. Even Nebuchadnezzar understood that God's "dominion is an everlasting dominion, and His kingdom endures from generation to generation" (Daniel 4:34). There is no "parenthesis," no gap of nearly two thousand years where God's dominion has somehow been put on hold.

First, it is equally obvious that the New Testament describes an approaching kingdom: "The kingdom of God is at hand" (Mark 1:14–15; Matthew 4:12–17). This means that there is a fuller expression of that already-present glorious kingdom approaching as God takes on human flesh and personally oversees the kingdom that brings with it the once-for-all sacrifice promised so long ago to Adam and Eve. The Seed of the woman, Jesus, has come to crush the head of the serpent (Genesis 3:15). "And when they had come to a place called Golgotha, which means Place of a Skull, [they] crucified Him" (Matthew 27:33–35). The head of the serpent was "crushed" as the stake of the cross penetrated the "skull" of the serpent. Because of the finished work of Jesus, through the power of His Spirit, Satan is crushed under *our* feet (Romans 16:20). The inaugurated kingdom becomes the expanding kingdom in time and in history prior to Jesus' return. The apostles are commanded to go into all the world and preach the gospel (Matthew

---

> **"The kingdom of God came upon the church of the first century, and there is no indication that it is being held in abeyance for a future millennium."**

28:18–20), a command not typical under the Old Covenant, although there were exceptions, as in Jonah preaching to the Ninevites. God's kingdom is not a political kingdom, and it will never be a political kingdom (John 18:36). Rather, the kingdom is "righteousness and peace and joy in the Holy Spirit" (Romans 14:17). But neither is this kingdom devoid of authority in this age: "For the kingdom of God does not consist in words, but in power" (1 Corinthians 4:20).

Second, there are verses that indicate that the kingdom *has come* and that it should affect the way we live in the world: (1) "For He delivered us from the domain of darkness, and transferred us to the kingdom of His beloved Son" (Colossians 1:13); (2) "Therefore, since we receive a kingdom which cannot be shaken, let us show gratitude, by which we may offer to God an acceptable service with reverence and awe" (Hebrews 12:28); (3) "I, John, your brother and fellow-partaker in the tribulation and kingdom and perseverance which are in Jesus, was on the island called Patmos, because of the word of God and the testimony of Jesus" (Revelation 1:9); (4) "And [Jesus] was saying to them, 'Truly I say to you, there are some of those who are standing here who shall not taste of death until they see the kingdom of God after it has come with power'" (Mark 9:1; Matthew 16:28; Luke 9:27); (5) "But if I cast out demons by the Spirit of God, then the kingdom of God has come upon you" (Matthew 12:28). "The truth is, Jesus *did* cast out demons by the Spirit of God."[2] The conclusion that we should reach is that the kingdom of God came upon the church of the first century, and there is no indication that it is being held in abeyance for a future millennium, often described as the "kingdom age."

Third, the kingdom requires new birth and sanctification to enter in (John 3:3; Matthew 7:21; 18:3) and prevents the unrighteous from entering (Matthew 5:20; 1 Corinthians 6:9–10; Ephesians 5:5). Yet, in another respect it contains even the wicked (Matthew 13:36–43). While the unrighteous live in the midst of God's kingdom, they do not have access to the King through His Mediator, Jesus Christ. Isn't this equally true of earthly kingships? While foreigners may reside within the borders of the United States, they do not have all the privileges of citizenship. For example, they cannot vote or run for political office. They do benefit, however, from the justice system under which citizens live.

Fourth, although Jesus states that the origination of His kingdom is heaven and not earth (John 18:36: "My kingdom is not of this world"), He nevertheless states that His kingdom is present, although it is different from all other kingdoms that manifest their power through military intrigue and force. Jesus speaks of "my kingdom" (18:36a). He claims to have His own "servants" (even though they do not fight with sword to defend Him [18:36b]). Jesus clearly asserts: "I am a king" (v. 37a). Finally, He confidently challenges Pilate: "For this I have been born, and for this I have come into the world, to bear witness to the truth" (18:37b).

Fifth, in Peter's Pentecost sermon we learn that Jesus suffered humiliation by enduring the curse of hanging "on a tree" (Galatians 3:13). But with His resurrection He began His exaltation in preparation for His ascension to the right hand of the throne of His Father, where He governs the universe with authority and power. There He was "crowned with glory and honor" (Hebrews 2:9) to begin His rule sitting at the right hand of God (Romans 8:34; Ephesians 1:20; Colossians 3:1; Hebrews 12:2; 1 Peter 3:22; Revelation 3:21) by wielding "all authority" (Matthew 28:18). By this authority Jesus promises to assist His people through "tribulation, or distress, or persecution, or famine, or nakedness, or peril, or sword" (Romans 8:34–35). In fact, He remains on that throne working for the collapse of all the works of His enemies (1 Corinthians 15:23–24; Hebrews 1:3, 13; 10:13).

Sixth, Christians have been raised up with Jesus as a testimony to our rule with Him (Ephesians 2:6). "We are, in the eyes of God, seated with Christ in heavenly places (which, in essence, is the idea of Revelation 20:4–6), i.e., in regal position."[3]

Restricting the Kingdom

Some believe the kingdom can only be identified within the confines of the church, and kingdom activity cannot manifest itself outside the church. In their view the kingdom is the church and nothing but the church. Since the church is "sacred" and the world "profane," as they see it, the church should not consider the world as an arena for kingdom activity. The world is the domain of the existing kingdoms which will only be judged when God's kingdom is inaugurated sometime in the future. Does this mean to hold a job in the world is to walk outside the kingdom?

> Perhaps the most common example of this restriction in Protestantism is found in *pietism*. Pietists restrict the kingdom of God to the sphere of personal piety, the inner life of the soul. . . . Other traditions curtail the scope of Christ's kingship by identifying the kingdom with the institutional church. . . . This view holds that only clergymen and missionaries engage in "full-time kingdom work" and that the laity are involved in kingdom activity only to the degree that they are engaged in church work. This restriction has given rise to the misleading phrase "church and world," which suggests that all of human affairs are in fact divided into two spheres.[4]

While the church has a particular function in the kingdom, the kingdom encompasses more than the church. "The institutional church is not to be equated with the kingdom of God. It is an agency of the kingdom, but it is not identical to the kingdom. The kingdom of God is as broad as the world."[5] When Jesus tells us to "seek first His kingdom and His righteousness" (Matthew 6:33), He reminds us that every earthly endeavor should be considered kingdom activity, whether family, church, business, or politics.

The Establishment of the Kingdom

Many Christians conclude that because the Bible describes a future kingdom that this is its sole emphasis. The kingdom cannot be presently with us if the kingdom is seen as yet to come. Actually, the kingdom is more than just a future reality. First, it is *definitively* established in the life, death, resurrection, and ascension of Jesus Christ. Second, it increases and advances *progressively* from that time to the end of the world. Third, it is established *fully* at Christ's second coming.

Definitive Establishment of the Kingdom

Let us first examine the definitive aspect of the kingdom.

Even a superficial reading of the gospels shows that the kingdom of God is the major theme of the ministries of both John the Baptist and Jesus. In fact, this is what the Gospels are all about: The King is coming to establish His kingdom. John the Baptist exhorted the people of Judea to repent because "the kingdom of heaven is *at hand*" (Matthew 3:2, emphasis added). From his very first sermon, Jesus preached a similar message: "Repent, for the kingdom of heaven is *at hand*" (Matthew 4:17, emphasis added). When Jesus sent out the seventy-two disciples, he told them to preach that "The kingdom of God has come *near* to you" (Luke 10:9, emphasis added).[6] The synoptic Gospels—Matthew, Mark, and Luke—all declare that the content of Jesus' entire teaching ministry can be summed up as the good news of the kingdom (Matthew 4:23; Mark 1:14–15; Luke 4:16–30; 4:43; 8:1). These passages, along with many others, prove that the establishment of the kingdom was imminent. It was "near" already in the time of Jesus.

There was, however, a very significant difference between the preaching of John and the preaching of Jesus. They often used the same words. But we find in Mark 1:15 that Jesus not only proclaims that the kingdom is near, but announces that "the time is fulfilled."[7] Thus, while John prophesied that it was almost time for the Lord to visit His people,

Jesus "asserted that this visitation was in actual progress, that God was already visiting his people."[8] Moreover, in Luke 17:21, Jesus tells the Pharisees that the "kingdom of God is in your midst."

Jesus also was establishing the kingdom by His works of healing. The clearest passages in this regard are Luke 4:21 and Matthew 11:2–6. Jesus quoted from the Old Testament prophecies of Isaiah about the

---

"While John prophesied that it was almost time for the Lord to visit His people, . . . Jesus tells the Pharisees that the 'kingdom of God is in your midst.' "

---

kingdom of God (Isaiah 35:5; 61:2), and in each case Jesus applied the prophecy to His works of healing and His teaching. In other words, Jesus claimed to be fulfilling the prophecies of the Old Testament. When the Pharisees charged Jesus with casting out demons by the power of the devil, He denied it, and added, "But if I cast out demons by the Spirit of God, *then the Kingdom of God has come upon you*" (Matthew 12:28). The verb used for "come upon" implies that something is present, not merely close by.[9] Jesus was saying that the casting out of demons demonstrated that the kingdom of God had arrived.

Jesus was establishing His rule by defeating the enemy of the kingdom, Satan. He gained the definitive victory over Satan supremely in His death on the cross and in His resurrection (Colossians 2:15; 1 Corinthians 15). But even during His earthly ministry, He was winning early skirmishes. The casting out of demons, a sign of the presence of the kingdom, was also a victory over Satan.

The definitive establishment of the kingdom takes place in several stages. Even in the initial establishment of the kingdom, a *principle of progress* is operating. The kingdom was dawning already when Christ was born. Throughout His life, He was routing enemy forces and extending His rule. His death was a triumph over Satan, and thus marked a further development in the founding of His kingdom. The Bible also says that Christ's kingdom is established by His resurrection. This was part of Peter's Pentecost message (Acts 2:32–36).

Finally, Christ's ascension is described in Scripture as an enthronement (Ephesians 1:20–23; Philippians 2:9–11). In Ephesians 1:21, Paul states explicitly that Christ has been placed "far above all rule and authority and power and dominion, and every name that is named, *not only in this age, but also in the one to come*" (emphasis added). This happened after God raised Jesus from the dead and "seated Him at His right hand in the heavenly places" (Ephesians 1:20). As A. A. Hodge said, "In the strictest sense we must date the actual and formal assumption of [Christ's] kingly office, in the full and visible exercise thereof, from the moment of His ascension into heaven from this earth and His session at the right hand of the Father."[10]

Progressive Advance of the Kingdom

The church is now engaged in the long-term extension of the kingdom: century after century of building, block by block. The *progressive* aspect of the kingdom is seen most clearly in Jesus' parables. In fact, one of the dominant notes of many parables is the progress of the kingdom. The kingdom of heaven is like a mustard seed that starts very small and grows into a huge tree, providing a resting place for the birds of the air (Matthew 13:31–32). The kingdom is also like leaven (yeast) placed in a loaf that eventually spreads throughout the loaf (Matthew 13:33). The parable of the wheat and tares also implies a progressive development of the kingdom. This is again a central feature of the parable. The owner of the field knows there are weeds in his wheat field, but he delays the harvest. He lets the wheat and the weeds grow and mature before he sends his laborers to harvest them (Matthew 13:24–30, 36–43).

What, then, did Jesus say would happen to the kingdom after its establishment? The parables cited above teach that the kingdom would grow. It began as a seed in a field, or as leaven in a loaf. Gradually, almost imperceptibly, it has grown into a tree and has leavened the whole lump. This same principle of permeation and growth and extension is found in many of the Old Testament prophecies of the kingdom.

Isaiah says that a child would be born a king, an obvious reference to the first advent of Christ. Once His kingdom is set up, there will be no

---

"The church is now engaged in the long-term extension of the kingdom. . . . Jesus will return to a world in which nearly all His enemies have been conquered."

---

end to the increase of His government and peace (Isaiah 9:2–7). It's not just that the kingdom is everlasting; its increase is everlasting. In Daniel 2, Nebuchadnezzar has a dream in which "the God of heaven [sets] up a kingdom which will never be destroyed" (Daniel 2:44–45). The kingdom is compared to a rock "cut out without hands" that becomes a great mountain and fills the whole earth (2:31–34). In the New Testament, in addition to the parables of Christ, Paul says that the end will come *after* "He has put all His enemies under His feet" (1 Corinthians 15:25), and that "the last enemy that will be abolished is death" (1 Corinthians 15:26). In other words, *Jesus will return to a world in which nearly all His enemies have been conquered.* The only enemy that will remain is death.

Final Manifestation of the Kingdom

The New Testament also teaches us to look for a future manifestation of the kingdom (Matthew 25; 1 Corinthians 15:23–24; Revelation 21). In this sense, the kingdom refers to heaven and the fullness of the new heavens and new earth. Our true and permanent home is in the heavenly mansion that Jesus is preparing for us. Our life here is a pilgrimage to that blessed land of rest. We look forward to heaven with joy and expectation, knowing that we shall be forever with our Savior and King in His perfect kingdom. The hope of heaven helps us endure the trials of the present life. We look forward to the day when all believers from all lands will gather to worship the Lamb that was slain from the beginning of the world, and when we will live in perfect peace and love, free from the last remnants of sin. Any Christian who does not eagerly await his heavenly reward is grievously confused. Any Christian whose *sole* hope is an earthly reward has not understood Christianity.

But this does not relieve us of responsibility on earth. On the last day, we will be judged according to our service on earth (Matthew 25). Thus, we cannot sit on our laurels and wait for Jesus to come. We must be seeking, and by His grace, working in the midst of Christ's kingdom throughout our lives as faithful subjects of the kingdom. Moreover, we do not look for a new kingdom. The heavenly kingdom is not something that God will establish for the first time at the end of history. It's simply the full, final, and glorious manifestation of the kingdom that was first established two thousand years ago. Since the coming of Christ, therefore, we can say that the kingdom is both *already* present in principle and *not yet* fully consummated.

12

"THERE IS A SEPARATION BETWEEN CHURCH AND STATE"

*Probably at the time of the adoption of the
Constitution, and of the Amendment to it
now under consideration, the general if not the
universal sentiment in America was, that
Christianity ought to receive encouragement
from the state, so far as was not incompatible
with the private rights of conscience and the
freedom of religious worship. An attempt to
level all religions, and to make it a matter of
state policy to hold all in utter indifference,
would have created universal disapprobation,
if not universal indignation.*

JOSEPH STORY

I n the U.S. Capitol building a room was set aside by the Eighty-third
Congress to be used exclusively for the private prayer and medita-
tion of Members of Congress. In this specially designated room there is
a stained-glass window showing George Washington kneeling in prayer.
Behind Washington a prayer is etched: "Preserve me, O God: for in
thee do I put my trust" (Psalm 16:1, KJV). The two lower corners of the

145

window each show the Holy Scriptures and an open book and a candle, signifying the light from God's law: "Thy word is a lamp unto my feet, and a light unto my path" (Psalm 119:105, KJV). Is this a violation of the First Amendment?

The highest office in our land demands the greatest wisdom. King Solomon learned this early in his political career, although he did not always follow it. American Presidents have had a high regard for the Bible because they knew that its wisdom was greater than what any man could offer.[1]

- **John Quincy Adams:** "The first and almost the only Book deserving of universal attention is the Bible. I speak as a man of the world . . . and I say to you, 'Search the Scriptures.'"

- **Abraham Lincoln:** "All the good from the Saviour of the world is communicated through this Book; but for the Book we could not know right from wrong. All the things desirable to man are contained in it."

- **Andrew Jackson:** "Go to the Scriptures. . . . [T]he joyful promises it contains will be a balsam to all your troubles."

- **Calvin Coolidge:** "The foundations of our society and our government rest so much on the teachings of the Bible that it would be difficult to support them if faith in these teachings would cease to be practically universal in our country."

- **Woodrow Wilson:** "The Bible . . . is the one supreme source of revelation of the meaning of life, the nature of God and spiritual nature and need of men. It is the only guide of life which really leads the spirit in the way of peace and salvation. . . . America was born a Christian nation. America was born to exemplify that devotion to the elements of righteousness which are derived from the revelations of Holy Scripture."

- **Harry S. Truman:** "The fundamental basis of this nation's law was given to Moses on the Mount. The fundamental basis of our Bill of Rights comes from the teachings we get from Exodus and St. Matthew, from Isaiah and St. Paul. I don't think we emphasize that enough these days. If we don't have the proper fundamental moral background, we will finally wind up with a totalitarian government which does not believe in right for anybody but the state."

Have these presidents violated the First Amendment? Did Congress violate the First Amendment when it declared 1983 to be "The Year of the Bible"?

The Bible, the Word of God, has made a unique contribution in shaping the United States as a distinctive and blessed nation. . . . [D]eeply held religious convictions springing from the Holy Scriptures led to the early settlement of our Nation. . . . [B]iblical teaching inspired concepts of civil government that are contained in our Declaration of Independence and the Constitution of the United States.[2]

The last sentence is interesting: "biblical teaching inspired concepts of civil government contained in . . . the Constitution." Are we to conclude that the Constitution is unconstitutional?

Shutting the Door on Christians

One way to keep Christians out of the public arena, especially politics, is to claim that there is a separation between church and state. The argument is based on the assumption that in biblical times church and

---

"One way to keep Christians out of the public arena, especially politics, is to claim that there is a separation between church and state."

---

state were merged. Supposedly priests ruled over elders, judges, and kings. If this is the case, so the argument goes, the Bible cannot be used in our modern pluralistic society where the Constitution forbids the state to be ruled by ecclesiastical officers. Caesar's realm is purely secular, using general revelation, natural law, or a simple majority of the citizenry as the standard for governing. Civil government, as these advocates see it, cannot turn to the Bible to develop a workable church/state relationship. As we will see, this scenario does not line up either with Scripture or the First Amendment to the Constitution.

What Do We Mean?

"Separation between church and state" means different things to different people. The most basic and legitimate definition is that the *institution* of the church is separate from the *institution* of civil government. The church as an institution cannot mingle in the institutional affairs of civil government. Neither can its officers. In the same way, civil government cannot disturb the ministry and operation of the church. This does not mean that laws having a religious foundation cannot be adopted and implemented by the state. For example, biblical laws against theft, murder, polygamy, abortion, homosexuality, and perjury have been accepted by civil governments as having a civil application with no transgression of the First Amendment. The state, however, does not have the jurisdictional right to compel people to believe the gospel, confess the true religion, pay tithes, or attend church. Neither can the civil magistrate declare any single Christian denomination to be the nationally established denomination.

Multiple Jurisdictions

The Bible teaches that there are multiple jurisdictions with specified functions and limits of authority and power: family, church, and state. Each jurisdiction has a biblically specified area or realm of operation. In Israel the Torah (Law) was used for all three jurisdictions. While the standard of law was the same—Torah—not all laws could be applied in the same way under each jurisdiction. For example, a father could discipline his own child for an infraction, but he could not discipline another family's child, excommunicate a church member, or inflict the death penalty on a criminal. While the state has the authority to try and execute convicted murderers, families and churches do not.

An elder in a church, in conjunction with other elders in his church, has ecclesiastical jurisdiction within his own church to discipline any member according to the guidelines laid down in Matthew 18 and to participate in proceedings to reconcile differences between fellow-believers (1 Corinthians 6). He cannot go to another church, however, and exercise discipline there (although he may be asked to sit in a judicial capacity, but only under the direction of the government of the church where the proceedings are taking place). Neither can he enter the jurisdiction of civil government as a representative of the church and use the power of the state to impose ecclesiastical laws upon the general citizenry.

None of this means that an individual church member cannot use the Bible to determine whether a candidate running for political office is fit for that office. While the Constitution states that no religious test can be given to someone seeking public office (possibly designed to keep denominational distinctives from being implemented),[3] this does not mean that individual voters cannot develop their own test.

Examples of Jurisdictional Separation

These principles have a long history, going back to the Old Testament era. Moses became the chief judicial officer in Israel, assisted by numerous lesser civil magistrates (Exodus 18:17–26). Aaron, Moses' brother, became the chief ecclesiastical officer as High Priest, assisted by numerous lesser priests (Exodus 29:1–9; Leviticus 8). Moses did not carry out the duties of a priest, and Aaron did not perform civil tasks.

In the days of the Judges, Othniel, Ehud, Shamgar, Gideon, and Samson served as political officers (Judges 1–13), while the son of Micah, Phineas, Eli, and the Levites served in an ecclesiastical capacity (Judges 17; 20:28; 1 Samuel 1–8).

During the period of the monarchy, King Saul served in a civil capacity while Ahimelech ministered as the chief ecclesiastical leader in the nation (1 Samuel 10 and 21). David was king while Abiathar carried out the priestly duties (1 Chronicles 15:11). David's son, Solomon, ruled as a civil officer while Zadok pursued the ecclesiastical obligations (1 Kings 1:45). Later, King Joash and Jehoiada the priest (2 Kings 11) and King Josiah and the priest Hilkiah (2 Kings 22:4) maintained jurisdictional separation. Even after the return from exile, church and state as parallel institutions operated with Governor Nehemiah (Nehemiah 7) and Priest Ezra (Nehemiah 8).

The following chart shows how the jurisdictional separation between church and state operated under the Old Covenant:

Civil	Ecclesiastical
Sword	Keys
Moses	Aaron
Elders	Levites
King	High Priest
Nehemiah	Ezra
Judah (and other tribes)	Levi

Jurisdictional Cooperation

In biblical terms, there was never such a separation between church and state that the state was free from following the guidelines of Scripture for its civil duties (Deuteronomy 17:18–20). Both priest and king were required to sit before the Law to be instructed. The priest was to follow guidelines pertaining to ecclesiastical affairs while the king would glean from Scripture those directives designed for his civil office. If a case was too difficult for the civil ruler to decide, the Bible gives the following instruction: "You shall come to the Levitical priest or the judge who is in office in those days, and you shall inquire of them, and they will declare to you the verdict in the case" (17:9). The Levites, as experts in the Law, were to assist the civil ruler, but the Levites were not called on to rule in place of the king. Consider the words of Psalm 2:10–12:

> Now therefore, O kings, show discernment; take warning, O judges of the earth. Worship the LORD with reverence, and rejoice with trembling. Do homage to the Son, lest He become angry, and you perish in the way, for his wrath may soon be kindled. How blessed are all who take refuge in Him!

The criteria for leadership in both church and state were based upon ethical considerations and previous governmental experience (Exodus 18:17–23; Deuteronomy 1:9–15 and 1 Timothy 3:1–7). The New Testament describes leaders in the church and state as ministers (Mark 10:42–45 and Romans 13:4). Even when describing the role of the civil magistrate, the Greek word for *deacon* or *servant* is used. The idea of a civil ruler as a minister is still with us. Men and women who work in the area of civil government are often described as "civil servants." The word underscores the ruler's duty to *serve* rather than to "lord it over" those under his authority. The civil "minister" rules for our good, and he is "an avenger who brings wrath upon the one who practices evil" (Romans 13:4).

King David did not dismiss the exhortation of the prophet Nathan after being confronted for his sins of adultery and murder. Although David at first did not know that the rebuke was levelled against him, he did not act as if it was unusual for someone of Nathan's position to seek the counsel of the king and even to offer the king advice. David accepted Nathan's rebuke. He did not tell Nathan that there is a "separation between church and state": "Then David said to Nathan, 'I have sinned against the LORD'" (2 Samuel 12:13).

Crossing the Boundaries

There is always the danger of jurisdictional usurpation, when, say, civil government removes the jurisdictional framework and enters the domain of the church. The Bible cites a number of examples of how the king sought to overrule the authority and jurisdiction of the church. King Saul assumed the duties of the priests when he offered sacrifices. He stepped out of the bounds of his kingly duties (1 Samuel 15:9–15, 22). In another place, King Saul killed the godly priest Ahimelech because he would not fulfill the king's political goals (1 Samuel 22:11–18). King Jeroboam established his state religion in Bethel and Dan. Non-Levites of the worst character were appointed to serve as priests (1 Kings 12:26–31).

King Uzziah is said to have been proud (2 Chronicles 26:16). His pride led him to go beyond his civil jurisdiction. While he was chief of state, being the king in Judah, he was not a priest. King Uzziah could not assume the role of a priest and perform ecclesiastical functions. He had no jurisdiction in the Temple. Uzziah ignored God's law and "acted corruptly, and he was unfaithful to the LORD his God, for he entered the temple of the LORD to burn incense on the altar of incense" (2 Chronicles 26:16).

God is serious about jurisdictional separation. The king was struck with the most feared disease in all Israel: leprosy. "And king Uzziah was a leper to the day of his death; and he lived in a separate house, being a leper, for he was cut off from the house of the LORD" (2 Chronicles 26:21). He lost access to the Temple, was isolated from the general population, and lost his kingdom to his son, Jotham, who "was over the king's house judging the people of the land" (26:21).

Azariah the priest was not passive in this whole affair. He knew the limitations of the king's power. He, along with "eighty priests of the LORD" (26:17), took action against the king. They opposed Uzziah the king, making it clear that "it is not for you, Uzziah, to burn incense to the LORD, but for the priests, the sons of Aaron who are consecrated to burn incense" (26:18). The priests commanded Uzziah to get out of the sanctuary.

These ecclesiastical officials are called valiant men (26:17) because they acted at great risk. While there were eighty of them, the king still commanded an army. He could have put them to death. There was a precedent for this when Ahimelech the priest helped David against King Saul (1 Samuel 21–22). King Saul called on Doeg the Edomite to attack the priests, after the king's own servants refused. "And Doeg the Edomite turned around and attacked the priests, and he killed that day eighty-five men who wore the linen ephod" (1 Samuel 22:18). Doeg the Edomite had no qualms about killing the priests. In our day, if our nation moves further from its biblical foundation, we'll see similar despisers who will rape the bride of Christ, the church. King Uzziah had Saul's hate in his eye: "Uzziah, with a censer in his hand for burning incense, was enraged" (2 Chronicles 26:19).

The priests were not casual about their duties. While they knew their lives were at stake, they were more concerned with the honor of the Lord (2 Chronicles 26:18); too often the church has been passive as the state has increasingly encroached on its ecclesiastical jurisdiction. The church forgets its God-ordained role. The church can deny its prophetic ministry when it is seduced by politics. Isn't this what happened when the people wanted to crown Jesus as King, to make Him their

---

"Jesus . . . is not a political Savior, but His saving work should affect politics."

---

political ruler? (John 6:15). They showed their true allegiance when Jesus refused to accept their view of what they thought God's kingdom should be like. "The distribution of bread moved the crowd to acclaim Jesus as the New Moses, the provider, the Welfare King whom they had been waiting for."[4] They were more interested in filling their bellies than saving their souls. When Jesus did not satisfy their false conception of salvation, they turned elsewhere: "We have no king but Caesar" (John 19:15). They denied the transforming work of the Holy Spirit to regenerate the dead heart of man. For them and for many today, man's salvation comes through political power. Jesus, however, is not a political Savior, but His saving work should affect politics.

What About the Constitution?

How many times have you heard someone say the reason Christians cannot be involved in proposing public policy is because the Constitution mandates a "separation between church and state"? The language of the separation between church and state translates into "Religion can have nothing to do with politics and anything politics touches." But few Americans have actually read the Constitution, and there's good reason to believe that only a small percentage of Americans have actually studied it. So it's not surprising that many people, Christians included, fail to recognize the following constitutional language:

Congress shall make no law respecting an establishment of religion, or prohibiting the free exercise thereof; or abridging the freedom of speech, or of the press; or the right of the people peaceably to assemble, and to petition the Government for a redress of grievances.

The following points can be made about the First Amendment:

- First, this amendment makes no mention of church or state.
- Second, there is no reference to a *separation* of church and state.
- Third, included in this amendment are items which relate to the "free exercise of religion" clause, but are typically ignored and narrowly applied: the right to talk about religion (freedom of speech), the right to publish religious works (freedom of the press), the right of people to worship publicly, either individually or in groups (freedom of assembly), and the right to petition the government when it goes beyond its delegated constitutional authority in these areas (the right of political involvement).
- Fourth, the prohibition is addressed to Congress, the only national law-making body in our nation. Individual states and governmental institutions (e.g., public schools, capitol building steps, national parks, etc.) are not included in the prohibition.
- Fifth, there is no mention of a freedom *from* religion, that is, people cannot protest and ask for the national government to outlaw religion just because it exists in the society in which they live or that it offends those of a different religion or who have no religion at all (atheists).

While the United States is rejecting its Christian heritage, former Communist regimes are adopting a more open view of the relationship between religion and politics. "Amid ongoing controversy, religious instruction has returned to Polish public schools" in the form of catechism instruction. "Lech Walesa, the Solidarity founder, told *Gazeta Wyborcza*, 'When communism has wrought such havoc I consider the teaching of religion as essential from a moral point of view. . . . The church is proposing to teach Poles, free of charge, honesty and morality.'"[5]

The First Amendment's History

With this introduction, let's look into the history and meaning of this much referred to but usually misquoted, misunderstood, and misapplied amendment. When the Constitution was sent to the states for ratification, there was fear that the new national government had too much power. It was then proposed that additional prohibitions should be listed in the Constitution to restrict further the national government's power and jurisdiction.

The area of religion was important since a number of the states had established churches. There was concern that a *national* church (e.g., Anglican, Presbyterian, or Congregational) would be funded by tax dollars and thus disestablish the existing state churches. So then, the First Amendment was designed to protect the states against national encroachment. The amendment was not designed to disestablish the Christian religion which predominated in the colonies. Justice Joseph Story, a Supreme Court justice of the nineteenth century, offers the following commentary on the amendment's meaning.

> The real object of the [F]irst Amendment was not to countenance, much less to advance Mohammedanism, or Judaism, or infidelity, by prostrating Christianity, but to exclude all rivalry among Christian sects [denominations] and to prevent any national ecclesiastical establishment which would give to an hierarchy the exclusive patronage of the national government.[6]

Story's comments are important. He states that the amendment's purpose was "to exclude all rivalry among Christian sects." This presupposes that Christianity was the accepted religion of the colonies but that no single denomination should be supported by the national government. The amendment was not designed to make all religions equal.

The word *establishment*, as used in the First Amendment, means recognition by government of a single denomination as the official church. The amendment prohibits not *the* establishment of religion (religion in general) but *an* establishment of religion (a Christian denomination in particular, which our founders called a "sect") by Congress. There is nothing in the First Amendment restricting the states.

If the amendment was constructed to remove religion from having even the slightest impact on civil governmental issues, then it seems rather strange that on September 24, 1789, the same day that it approved the First Amendment, Congress called on President Washington to proclaim a national day of prayer and thanksgiving. The First Congress resolved:

> That a joint committee of both Houses be directed to wait upon the President of the United States to request that he would recommend to the people of the United States a day of public thanksgiving and prayer, to be observed by acknowledging, with grateful hearts, the many signal favors of Almighty God, especially by affording them an opportunity peaceably to establish a Constitution of government for their safety and happiness.

This proclamation acknowledges "the many signal favors of Almighty God, especially by *affording them an opportunity peaceably to establish a Constitution of government for their safety and happiness*" (emphasis added). This is rather strange language for a group of men who supposedly just separated religion from government at all levels, a government they would not have had if God had not made it possible.

The First Congress also established the congressional chaplain system by which official daily prayers to God are still offered. In the entire debate on the First Amendment, not one word was said by any congressman about a "wall of separation between church and state." At the time of the drafting of the First Amendment, a number of the thirteen colonies had established churches.

> At the beginning of the Revolution established churches existed in nine of the colonies. . . . The first amendment in large part was a guarantee to the states which insured that the states would be able to continue whatever church-state relationship existed in 1791. Maryland, Virginia, North Carolina, South Carolina, and Georgia all shared Anglicanism as the established religion common to those colonies. Congregationalism was the established religion in Massachusetts, New Hampshire, and Connecticut. New York, on the other hand, allowed for the establishment of Protestant religions. Only in Rhode Island and Virginia were all religious sects disestablished. But all of the States still retained the Christian religion as the foundation stone of their social, civil, and political institutions. Not even Rhode Island and Virginia renounced Christianity, and both states continued to respect and acknowledge the Christian religion in their system of law.[7]

A summary reading of some of the state constitutions will easily prove this point. Notice the dates when these state constitutions were

---

"There was nothing unconstitutional in having a state endorse a particular religion."

---

still in effect. There was nothing unconstitutional in having a state endorse a particular religion. All fifty states of the United States express dependence on Almighty God for their perseverance and strength.[8] Older versions of these constitutions are even more explicit about the Christian faith. Here are several examples:

The Connecticut Constitution (until 1818): "The People of this State . . . by the Providence of God . . . hath the sole and exclusive right of governing themselves as a free, sovereign, and independent State . . . and forasmuch as the free fruition of such liberties and privileges as humanity, civility, and Christianity call for us, as is due to every man in his place and proportion . . . hath ever been, and will be the tranquility and stability of Churches and Commonwealth; and the denial thereof, the disturbances, if not the ruin of both."

The Delaware Constitution (1831): ". . . no man ought to be compelled to attend any religious worship. . . ." It recognizes "the duty of all men frequently to assemble together for the public worship of the Author of the Universe." The following oath of office was in force until 1792: "I . . . do profess faith in God the Father, and in Jesus Christ His only Son, and in the Holy Ghost, one God, blessed for evermore; I do acknowledge the holy scriptures of the Old and New Testaments to be given by divine inspiration."

The Maryland Constitution (until 1851): "That, as it is the duty of every man to worship God in such a manner as he thinks most acceptable to him; all persons professing the Christian religion, are equally entitled to protection in their religious liberty. . . . The Legislature may, in their discretion, lay a general and equal tax, for the support of the Christian religion." The constitution of 1864 required "a declaration of a belief in the Christian religion" for all state officials.

The North Carolina Constitution (1876): "That no person who shall deny the being of God, or the truth of the Protestant religion, or the divine authority of the Old or New Testaments, or who shall hold religious principles incompatible with the freedom and safety of the State, shall be capable of holding any office or place of trust or profit in the civil department within this State."

Since the First Amendment prohibits Congress from establishing a religion, the states were free from national control when it came to religious issues. Today's courts have reinterpreted the First Amendment to mean that any law that has any religious foundation is unconstitutional. For example, if a school teaches that abstinence is the best method to prevent pregnancy, or that premarital sex is immoral, and such views are the teaching of major religions (Protestants and Catholics), then abstinence cannot be taught in a public school.

Historical Fiction

The present church/state debate is historical fiction. The origin of the "separation between church and state" phrase can be found in the writings of Roger Williams, founder of Rhode Island, and in a letter Thomas Jefferson wrote to a group of Baptist pastors in Danbury, Connecticut, in 1802. Jefferson's use of the phrase, "a mere metaphor too vague to support any theory of the Establishment Clause,"[9] has been adopted as the standard interpretation of the First Amendment. If the constitutional framers had wanted to use Williams's phraseology (later picked up by Jefferson), they could have done so. Instead, they chose a more specific phraseology to convey a specific meaning.

The meaning, as history will attest, had nothing to do with separating the moral aspects of religion as they relate to civil issues from state affairs as the Northwest Ordinance of 1787 attests: "Religion, morality and knowledge, being necessary to good government and the happiness of mankind, schools and the means of education shall be forever encouraged." As constitutional scholar Leo Pfeffer writes: "[F]or all practical purposes Christianity and religion were synonymous . . . ."[10]

Our founders, Jefferson included, never supposed that moral precepts founded on religion were to be excluded from policy making:

> Jefferson's own conception of the wall of separation between church and state did not prevent him from advocating and implementing government for religious education in the state of Virginia. After he retired as President, Jefferson wrote a bill for Virginia providing for the creation of public elementary schools, which the state passed in 1817. The bill provided that "no religious reading, instruction or exercise, shall be prescribed or practiced *inconsistent with the tenets of any religious sect or denomination.*" This law still allowed nondenominational religious activities.[11] (emphasis added)

Jefferson's Bible, also known as "The Morals of Jesus," was a compilation of "the very words of Jesus." Jefferson stated that "there will be found remaining the most sublime and benevolent code of morals

---

"The present church/state debate is historical fiction. . . . Our founders, Jefferson included, never supposed that moral precepts founded on religion were to be excluded from policy making."

---

which has ever been offered to man."[12] So, what was designed to keep the national government from establishing a national church is now being interpreted to keep even religious precepts from entering the realm of politics.

The Treaty of Tripoli

An issue that continues to be put forward as incontrovertible evidence that our founders self-consciously denied any attachment to the Christian religion, and that there is a radical separation between religion and civil government, is the Treaty of Tripoli (1797). Article 11 of the treaty reads:

> As the government of the United States of America *is not in any sense founded on the Christian religion,*—as it has in itself no character of enmity against the law, religion or tranquility of Musselmen,—and as the said States never have entered into any war or act of hostility against any Mehomitan nation, it is declared by the parties that no pretext arising from religious opinions shall ever produce an interruption of the harmony existing between the two countries. (emphasis added)

The treaty has been attributed to the work and beliefs of George Washington numerous times. A portion of the above quotation found its way to the cover of *Liberty Magazine*. The publisher gave the impression that George Washington wrote it. Washington's signature followed the excerpted line that read, "The United States of America is not in any sense founded on the Christian religion." As we will see, this is inaccurate and deceptive.

The Encyclopedia of Philosophy concocts a story of how George Washington "acquiesced" to the radical deistic views of Joel Barlow, then American consul in Algiers. Here is the story:

> In answer to a direct question from a Muslim potentate in Tripoli, Washington acquiesced in the declaration of Joel Barlow, then American Consul in Algiers, that "the government of the United States of America is not in any sense founded on the Christian religion."[13]

From reading this, one gets the impression that Washington went to Tripoli and had a conversation with the Muslim potentate where he answered a question relating to America's religious foundation. This is pure fiction. Joel Barlow was the culprit, borrowing heavily from Thomas Paine. Washington had nothing to do with the treaty. He had left office before the treaty was signed.

Norman Geisler, author of *Is Man the Measure: An Evaluation of Contemporary Humanism,* uncritically accepts the *Encyclopedia of Philosophy*'s conclusion concerning the Treaty of Tripoli and George Washington's part in it. He states that:

> Our nation's founders were largely humanistic (or deistic). . . . There were few evangelical Christians among the signers of the Declaration

of Independence, John Witherspoon being a notable exception. And when George Washington was asked if the United States was a Christian country, he replied that "the government of the United States of America is not in any sense founded on the Christian religion."[14]

Geisler offers no evidence of Washington ever being asked this question.

During the 1984 presidential elections, People for the American Way (PAW), aired a commercial on a national television cable station, titled "Founding Fathers/Separation of Church and State." Noted actor Martin Sheen narrated. Sheen said: "Today the voices evoking religious dogma have invaded the highest places of government, challenging the ideas of our Founding Fathers and the separation of church and state." What did People for the American Way use to support this claim of the views of the Founding Fathers? PAW turned to a chopped quotation from the Treaty of Tripoli and maintained that they were the words of George Washington. Sheen continued: "'The government of the United States,' insisted Washington, 'is not in any sense founded on the Christian religion or any other religion.'" PAW cannot even misquote with integrity. Nowhere does the Treaty of Tripoli contain the words "or any other religion."

Jim Castelli, in a syndicated newspaper article titled "'Christian America': A Myth Keeps Living On" (July 4, 1984), attaches John Adams's name to the infamous words. President Adams did sign the treaty on June 10, 1797, three days after it was passed by the Senate. John Adams was not shy about his faith. If he did sign the treaty with the disputed passage, then his actions were out of accord with what he considered to be America's beliefs. This is evident in his "Proclamation for a National Fast Day" on March 6, 1799:

> I have thought proper to recommend, and I hereby recommend accordingly, that Thursday, the twenty-fifth day of April next, be observed throughout the United States of America as a day of solemn humiliation, fasting, and prayer; that the citizens on that day abstain, as far as may be, from their secular occupation, and devote the time to the sacred duties of religion, in public and in private; that they call to mind our numerous offences against the most high God, confess them before him with the sincerest penitence, implore his pardoning mercy,

through the Great Mediator and Redeemer, for our past transgressions, and that through the grace of His Holy Spirit, we may be disposed and enabled to yield a more suitable obedience to his righteous requisitions in time to come . . .

On another occasion, John Adams wrote: "The general principles, on which the Fathers achieved independence, were . . . the general principles of Christianity."[15] How then do we reconcile Adams's public remarks about Christianity with the Treaty of Tripoli? It's possible that the treaty is nothing more than a pronouncement "that 'the Christian religion' as a formal institution was not a part of the American government in the same way that the religious structures of Islam are a part of Islamic governments. From many things that Adams and his contemporaries wrote it is clear that they did not use the word *religion* to exclude Christian ideas or principles as some do today. True, the founders did not make institutional religion a part of the government. But they never thought of excluding Christian principles."[16]

A Question of Authenticity

There is some question concerning the authenticity of the 1796 treaty. Constitutional lawyer John W. Whitehead maintains "that the Treaty of Tripoli is a mysterious, confusing and often misinterpreted document. Since the records of the Treaty negotiations of 1796–1797 are incomplete, many of the questions surrounding the treaty appear to be unanswerable."[17]

Joel Barlow oversaw the translation process from Arabic to English. In 1930 the original Arabic version was retranslated into English by Dr. C. Snouck Hurgronje of Leiden. Barlow's translation and Dr. Hurgronje's retranslation bear a faint resemblance to each other. For example, in Article 12 of Barlow's version, all religious references have been removed: "Praise be to God!"; "May God strengthen [the Pashna of Tripoli], and the Americans"; "May God make it all permanent love and a good conclusion between us"; and, "by His grace and favor, amen!"

The deception does not stop with Article 12. It seems that there was even more tampering with the document in its translation process. Was Barlow the culprit?

Most extraordinary (and wholly unexplained) is the fact that Article 11 of the Barlow translation with its famous phrase, "the government of the United States of America is not in any sense founded on the Christian religion," does not exist at all. There is no Article 11. . . . How that script came to be written and to be regarded, as in the Barlow translation, as Article 11 of the treaty as there written, is a mystery and seemingly must remain so. Nothing in the diplomatic correspondence of the time throws any light whatever on the point.[18]

The infamous phrase seems to be nonexistent in the original treaty. With Barlow's ties with the anti-Christian Thomas Paine, it should not surprise us that he would tamper with the document.

The 1805 Treaty

There were two treaties with Tripoli. The 1796 treaty gets all the attention while the 1805 revised treaty is ignored by the critics. It is important to note that the 1805 treaty with Tripoli differs considerably from the 1796 version (ratified June 7, 1797). The most important difference is this: In the 1805 version, the phrase "as the Government of the United States of America is not in any sense founded on the Christian religion" is conspicuously absent. Barlow had no part in the second treaty. The first treaty was terminated by war. A new treaty was drafted in 1805 (ratified April 12, 1806). Article 14 of the new treaty corresponds to Article 11 of the first treaty: "The government of the United States of America has in itself no character of enmity against the laws, religion, or tranquility of Musselmen. . . ." The sentence in dispute does not appear.

If the critics of a Christian America thesis are going to be honest, then they must give an adequate reason why the revised 1805 treaty does not contain the words that seem to denounce the Christian religion. They also must answer why the revised treaty occurred during Thomas Jefferson's term as president!

George Washington stated that "it is the duty of all nations to acknowledge the providence of Almighty God, to obey His will, to be grateful for His benefits, and humbly to implore His protection and favor." He went on in his Thanksgiving Proclamation of October 3, 1789, to write that as a nation "we may then unite in most humbly offering our prayers and supplications to the great Lord and Ruler of Nations, and beseech Him to pardon our national and other transgressions."

If treaties are going to establish the religious commitment of the nation, then it is essential that we look at all of the treaties. In 1822, The United States, along with Great Britain and Ireland, ratified a "Convention for Indemnity Under Award of Emperor of Russia as to the True Construction of the First Article of the Treaty of December 24, 1814." It begins with these words: "In the name of the Most Holy and Indivisible Trinity." Only Christianity teaches a trinitarian view of God. If the Treaty of Tripoli does in fact make Christianity null and void (which it does not), based on the logic of the critics, the Treaty of 1822 reestablishes it.[19]

"GOD'S KINGDOM IS NOT OF THIS WORLD"

*By "not of this world" we are to understand
that the nature and origin of His kingdom
are not of this world, not that His kingdom
will not extend in this world. In the world's
sense of king and kingdom, in the sense in
which the Roman empire claimed to rule the
world, He had no kingdom.*

H. W. WATKINS

Cousin America has eloped with a Presbyterian parson," Horace Walpole wrote in 1775. While Walpole does not name the parson, many believe that he had John Witherspoon in mind. Like all Christians of his era, Witherspoon regarded civil government as a subordinate institution under God's all-embracing kingdom (Isaiah 9:6–7).

Witherspoon and other Christian patriots of his era had no delusions about "bringing in God's kingdom" through political maneuvering. They recognized, as Benjamin Franklin so eloquently stated at the Constitutional Convention: "God governs in the affairs of men." God governs because He is King, and this world is part of His universal kingdom-realm. While His kingdom is not *of* this world, it certainly operates *in* and *over* this world. Franklin continued:

And if a sparrow cannot fall to the ground without his notice [Matthew 10:29], is it probable that an empire can rise without his aid? We have been assured . . . in the sacred writings that "except the Lord build the house, they labor in vain that build it" [Psalm 127:1]. I firmly believe this, and I also believe that without his concurring aid we shall succeed in this political building no better than the builders of Babel.

The kingdoms of men are dependent upon the operation of the Kingdom of God in and over this world. Birds do not fall and kingdoms do not rise without the rule of God's providential hand.

More than a century before the drafting of the Declaration of Independence, John Eliot, the Puritan missionary to the Indians, wrote in his *The Christian Commonwealth* (a document intended as a plan of government for the Natick Indian community) that it is not for man

> to search humane Polities and Platformes of Government, contrived by the wisdom of man; but as the Lord hath carried on their works for them, so they ought to go unto the Lord, and enquire at the Word of his mouth, what Platforme of Government he hath therein commanded; and humble themselves to embrace that as the best. . . . [The] written Word of God is the perfect System or Frame of Laws, to guide all the Moral actions of man, either towards God or man.[1]

Because we are living in God's kingdom, Eliot taught, it is our duty to follow the King's rules.

It was still the responsibility of the citizenry, as subjects of the King of heaven, to bring about a civil government that meets the conditions of heaven:

> I would neither have you trust in an arm of flesh nor sit with folded hands and expect miracles should be wrought in your defence. This is a sin which is in Scripture styled tempting God.[2]

To trust in politics—"an arm of flesh"—was to trust in a kingdom that derived its power from this world. It was this misplaced trust, a preoccupation of pagan Rome, that led Jesus to proclaim, "My kingdom is not of this world" (John 18:36). God's kingdom should not be made in the image of Roman political theory.

The Kingdom and the Kingdoms

If Jesus' kingdom is not of this world, so the argument goes, then how can Christians claim to have a responsibility to be involved in working for the kingdom? Since God's kingdom is exclusively heavenly, as some assert, there can be no earthly manifestation of God's works other than redeeming the lost. God's kingdom has nothing to do with this world until He personally reigns on this earth in the millennium; this is the refrain of much of modern-day fundamentalism. These are typical responses given to the person who asks, "Why aren't you more involved in bringing about reformation in the world?" As we have already seen, there is more to God's kingdom than an exclusively heavenly reign or even a literal thousand-year rule of Christ on the earth.

Some Christian writers are so extreme in their insistence that God's kingdom does not touch on earthly things that they are even denying that Jesus' millennial reign is the kingdom of God. Dave Hunt, a proponent of an any moment rapture, wrote that "the millennial reign of Christ, *far from being the kingdom*, is actually the final proof of the incorrigible nature of the human heart."[3] Hunt later retracted this statement,[4] but his further writings on the same subject leave a clear impression: The kingdom cannot be manifested in a world where sinners still have bodies of flesh and blood:

> While [the kingdom] does have an earthly manifestation during the millennium, the kingdom will not be realized in its eternal fullness— which "flesh and blood cannot inherit" (1 Corinthians 15:50)—except in the new indestructible and incorruptible universe that will be created after the present one is destroyed.[5]

Dave Hunt and others appeal to John 18:36 ("My kingdom is not of this world") to establish that the kingdom is essentially (exclusively?) a heavenly and inner reality.[6] David Wilkerson quotes this passage and adds, "That settles it for me, as it should for all believers who tremble at His Word."[7] We must, as Wilkerson says, take Christ's words with the utmost seriousness. The question is, what does Christ's statement mean? What is settled by a recitation of a single verse with no context?

What does Jesus mean when he tells Pilate that His kingdom is not of this world? Does He mean that His kingdom is like the invisible ether that scientists a century ago believed pervaded outer space? Does He mean that His kingdom has no effect on the course of history? Quoting the verse without explanation does little to enhance our understanding of the exchange of words between the inquisitor and the accused. It doesn't settle anything to quote a passage without study.

That Little Preposition

Several important issues need to be discussed to arrive at a proper interpretation of John 18:36. Perhaps the most important question to answer is what the preposition *of* (Greek, *ek*) means. This may seem obvious, but it is not. Just think of how many different ways we use *of* in English: The Queen of England (tells us the Queen's domain), a stack of wood (tells what kind of stack), a box of cereal (tells the contents of the box), etc. Greek has the same kind of variety. Essentially, it means "out of," and it can have several shades of meaning: separation, the direction from which something comes, source or origin, as well as a host of minor meanings.[8] Many commentators agree that in John 18:36 *ek* has the sense of "source"; thus, Jesus' statement has to do with the *source* of His kingdom authority and power.

The French commentator Godet wrote, "The expression *ek tou kosmou, of this world,* is not synonymous with *en to kosmo, in this world.* For the kingdom of Jesus is certainly realized and developed here on earth; but it does not have its *origin* from earth, from the human will and earthly force."[9]

More recently, the Lutheran commentator R. C. H. Lenski has written, "The origin of Jesus' kingdom explains its unique character: it is 'not of this world.' . . . [All other kingdoms] sprang out of [*ek*] this world and had kings that corresponded to such an origin."[10] B. F. Westcott agrees that Jesus meant that His kingdom "does not derive its origin or its support from earthly forces. . . . At the same time Christ's kingdom is 'in the world,' even as His disciples are ([John] xvii.11)."[11] Charles Ryrie's study Bible explains that Jesus meant that His kingdom is "not of human origin."[12] Robert Culver comments in *Toward a Biblical View of Civil Government,*

The words "of this world" translate *ek tou kosmou toutou,* that is, out of this world. Source rather than realm is the sense. . . . The future consummation of the kingdom of Christ cannot rightly be said to be beyond history. No indeed! It will occur in history and is history's goal. . . . So Jesus very clearly is making no comment on either the nature of his kingdom or His realm, rather on the power and source of its establishment.[13]

Thus, when Jesus said that His kingdom is not "of" this world, He meant that it does not *derive its authority and power from the world;* His kingdom is from another place. This verse refers to the *origin* of the

---

"When Jesus said that His kingdom is not 'of' this world, He meant that it does not derive its authority and power from the world; His kingdom is from another place."

---

kingdom, not to its *location* in the universe. Jesus was not saying that His kingdom floats in the air, without touching the world. He did not mean that He rules heaven, but has left earth to be ruled by Satan. Rather, He meant that His rule has its *origin* in heaven, not in the world.

Pilate's Perspective

Pilate's question about kingship and kingdoms concerned political power as he, an earthly ruler from Rome, understood it. Since Pilate's question emerged from Pilate's perspective, Jesus answered in a way that Pilate understood. In John 18:37 Pilate says, "So You are a king?" Jesus did not deny kingship. Jesus answered Pilate's tentative question forthrightly: "You say correctly that I am a king. For this I have been born

[Luke 1:32–33; 2:2], and for this I have come into the world, to bear witness to the truth. Every one who is of the truth hears My voice" (John 18:37). Would Jesus bring an army? How large would it be? Since He was said to be "King of the Jews" (Luke 23:3), would Jesus incite a rebellion among the Jews to usurp Pilate's position of authority? What sort of weaponry would He use? Pilate believed, as did many Jews of that day, that armed conflict alone could extend a kingdom. It was a king's duty to use the power of the military against an enemy. Since Jesus was a king, Pilate assumed He must command His army in the same way. This was the Roman way:

> The reader is presented with a dramatic scene, in which two types of kingships are contrasted; the kingship backed by the authority and might of imperial Rome represented by Pilate, a kingship *of this world* and upheld by this world's weapons, and the kingship of Jesus *not of this world*, in which the monarch is to reign by being lifted up on a cross ([John 18:]36). The narrative clearly presupposes that it had been intimated to Pilate that Jesus, by claiming kingship over Jewry, was in effect a political revolutionary and therefore a potential danger to Rome. . . .[14]

Later, Jesus informed Pilate that his own position of political authority, and, by intimation, that of all who rule (Romans 13:1), was subject to God's kingly authority since Jesus is "ruler of the kings of the earth" (Revelation 1:5).

When Jesus kept silent in response to Pilate's question concerning His origin (John 19:9), Pilate grew indignant: "You do not speak to me? Do you not know that I have authority to release You, and I have authority to crucify you?" (19:10). Jesus' answer settled the matter about the operation of God's kingdom. Unless the kingdom of God operated *in* and *over* this world, what Jesus said next would be false: "You would have no authority over Me, unless *it had been given you from above.* . . ." (19:11, emphasis added).

So then, God's kingdom does operate in this world. So much so that it influences the kingdoms of men: "The king's heart is like channels of water in the hand of the LORD; He turns it wherever He wishes" (Proverbs 21:1). It's no wonder that Pilate said that he found no guilt in Jesus deserving death (Luke 23:22).

Confusion over Jesus' words develops from a false notion that the answer to man's problems is solely political. There were numerous occasions when the crowds wanted to make Him king (John 6:15). While there are political implications to Jesus' kingship, just as there are per-

---

"God's kingdom does operate in this world. So much so that it influences the kingdoms of men."

---

sonal, familial, economic, business, ecclesiastical, and judicial implications, the kingdom of God is not brought about politically. Good laws do not make good people. Only the sovereign work of the Holy Spirit in regeneration makes people good. The state has a God-imposed jurisdiction to perform activities to promote the kingdom according to the specifics of God's Word as they relate to civil matters.

The people in Jesus' day saw the kingdom of God only in externals. They visualized the kingdom of God as coming, not through regeneration, but by revolution. Jesus said of His followers: "Truly, truly, I say to you, you seek Me, not because you saw signs, but because you ate of the loaves, and were filled" (John 6:26). It was Jesus' message about mankind's need for salvation and about Him as the Savior, the Messiah of God, that caused the religious and political establishments of the day to seek His death.

The kingdom of God never advances through political intrigue backed by military power. Though power-directed, the kingdom's power comes from above and works on the heart of man: "I will give you a new heart and put a new spirit within you; and I will remove the heart of stone from your flesh and give you a heart of flesh. And I will put My Spirit within you and cause you to walk in My statutes, and you will be careful to observe My ordinances" (Ezekiel 36:26–27). Self-government, wherein God subdues the heart to teachableness, leads to godly family, church, and civil governments (1 Timothy 3:1–13).

Implements of war which deteriorate over time or become obsolete are only as reliable as those who manufacture and use them. Moreover, such weapons affect only externals. They can subdue a people, but they cannot regenerate those dead in their trespasses and sins (Ephesians 2:1). God's Word, on the other hand, "is living and active and sharper than any two-edged sword, and piercing as far as the division of soul and spirit, of both joints and marrow, and able to judge the thoughts and intentions of the heart" (Hebrews 4:12).

The supernatural power which energizes God's kingdom is never bound by political rhetoric: "For the kingdom of God does not consist in words, but in power" (1 Corinthians 4:20). The battle against the kingdoms of this world is waged through the awesome power inherent in God's Word, energized by His Spirit: "For though we walk in the flesh, we do not war according to the flesh, for the weapons of our warfare are not of the flesh, but divinely powerful for the destruction of fortresses" (2 Corinthians 10:3–4). It is the power of regeneration, not revolution, that advances the kingdom.

As Christians, "we are destroying speculations and every lofty thing raised up against the knowledge of God, and we are taking every thought captive to the obedience of Christ" (2 Corinthians 10:5). This is living for the kingdom in the power of God's Spirit. The kingdom of God advances by changing the hearts and minds of those who oppose Jesus Christ and His Word. The kingdoms of this world are at war with the kingdom of Jesus Christ, and it is the duty of all Christians to be involved in that war until the gates of Hades no longer stand (Matthew 16:18).

Restoration begins by realizing that we live in the midst of God's kingdom. God's pattern for godly living is established in heaven. In the Lord's Prayer we petition God, "Thy Kingdom come. Thy will be done, *on earth as it is in heaven*" (Matthew 6:10, emphasis added).

Some Objections

There are some Christians who maintain that the kingdom parables of Matthew 13 teach a different view of the kingdom from the one expressed above. They go to great lengths to try to prove that God's kingdom has little or virtually no positive effect on this world prior to His

Second Coming. J. Dwight Pentecost, representing a school of interpretation known as dispensational premillennialism, believes that the kingdom loses its effectiveness over time, is a monstrosity, and is like evil. Let's put his views to the test.

The Parable of the Sower and the Soils

In comments on the parable of the soils in Matthew 13:1–9, Pentecost states that "During the course of the age there will be a *decreasing* response to the sowing of the seed, from 'a hundredfold' to 'sixty' to 'thirty.'"[15] This is an odd interpretation seeing that one seed results in at least thirty *additional* seeds, not to mention an increase of sixty and one hundred. A thirty-to-one return on an investment is very impressive. Pentecost understands this parable to teach that the kingdom declines in influence over time. This is off the mark.

A careful reading of the text shows that the seeds are thrown at the same time (Matthew 13:4), and at maturation all the seeds produce in varying amounts—some produce a hundred more, some sixty more, and others "only" thirty more. The point is in the abundance of growth. "The Lord is not informing His disciples of the *decline* of gospel influence, but of its *increase*,"[16] up to one hundred to one!

Pentecost sees something significant in the *order*, from an increase of one hundred to one to a decrease of thirty to one. But if we look at the same parable in Mark 4:1–9, we soon learn that as the seeds "grew up and increased, they were yielding a crop and were producing thirty, sixty, and a hundredfold" (4:8). Here the order is reversed! If we assert that the order of increase tells us something about the maturation of the kingdom, then the parable in Mark tells us that the kingdom will advance beyond anything we could ever imagine, just the opposite of what Matthew teaches. The order is not the point; it is the amount of increase that God wants us to learn from the parable.

The Parable of the Mustard Seed

In this parable Jesus contrasts the tiny mustard seed with its potential for growth: from "smaller than all other seeds" to "larger than the garden plants," large enough so "the birds of the air come and nest in its branches" (Matthew 13:31–32). Pentecost states, based on the teaching of this parable, that this age, prior to the return of Christ, "is characterized by an abnormal external growth. That which was to be an herb has become a tree—it has developed into a monstrosity."[17] This is an unbelievable interpretation. There is no indication that Jesus is describing God's kingdom as a monstrosity. It's only a monstrosity to those who fail to see the plain meaning of the text.

Again, like the parable of the sower and the soils, this parable is comparing the relatively small seed with its enormous growth capacity, because it is a description of God's kingdom. We should expect big things to happen when God is the one who brings about the growth (1 Corinthians 3:6–7). Jesus often used this type of comparative language to demonstrate how God uses the seemingly insignificant things to accomplish great things. Paul picks up on this theme when he describes how God "has chosen the foolish things of the world to shame the wise, and God has chosen the weak things of the world to shame the things which are strong" (1 Corinthians 1:27). In another place, the apostle shows how weakness, when it is acknowledged before God, is actually strength: "For when I am weak, then I am strong" (2 Corinthians 12:10).

Jesus uses the mustard seed in another place to demonstrate the principle of smallness in kind but bigness in result: "For truly I say to you, if you have faith as a mustard seed, you shall say to this mountain, 'Move from here to there,' and it shall move; and nothing shall be impossible" (Matthew 17:20).

The interpretation turns ridiculous when Pentecost wants us to believe that the birds in the parable are types of evil because in the first parable they ate the seeds that fell beside the road (Mark 4:4). But are birds always types of evil? God is said to feed the birds in Matthew 6:26. Does this mean that God is feeding evil? In the first parable the birds eat the seed; in this parable they nest in the tree's branches. These are two different actions. Nesting seems to be a good thing (Matthew 8:20). The imagery of birds nesting in the branches of a tree is based on Ezekiel 17:22–24. Birds nesting in the branches of a tree is a blessed thing: "And birds of every kind will nest under it; they will nest in the shade of its branches" (17:23).

The Parable of the Leaven

To avoid the implication that God's kingdom will advance in history prior to Jesus' second coming, the kingdom of God becomes evil. Pentecost tells us that "the figure [of leaven] is used in Scripture to portray that which is evil in character."[18] Since Scripture says that "The king-

---

"There is no getting around it. God's kingdom is with us, and it will continue with us."

---

dom of heaven is like leaven" (Matthew 13:33), and Pentecost maintains that leaven is used to portray that which is evil, then the parable must be teaching that the kingdom is like evil.

There are a number of places in Scripture where leaven is a symbol of invisible evil influence (Matthew 16:6, 11; 1 Corinthians 5:7–8; Galatians 5:9). Does this mean that every use of leaven in Scripture is a reference to evil? If this principle applies in this instance, then it must apply in all instances. The results are not too encouraging.

> The figurative language of Scripture is not so stereotyped, that one figure must always stand for one and the same thing. The devil is 'a roaring *lion*, seeking whom he may devour' (1 Pet. v. 8); yet this doesn't hinder the same title from being applied to Christ, 'the *Lion* of the tribe of Judah' (Rev. v. 5); only there the subtlety and fierceness of the animal formed the point of comparison, there the nobility and kingliness and conquering strength.[19]

Consider another example. Satan is depicted as a serpent (Genesis 3:1; 2 Corinthians 11:3; Revelation 12:9; 20:2). God's people are told to be "shrewd as serpents." How are we to understand what the Bible means when it tells us to be "shrewd as serpents"? One way is to take a narrow definition based on its association with Satan. Satan is depicted as a serpent, and he is evil. In the same way, Christians are to be shrewd in an evil sense like the devil. This is not what Jesus had in mind. Here's another example of choosing a definition of serpent in a narrow, one-meaning sense. The bronze serpent is a type of Christ (Numbers 21:9): "And as Moses lifted up the serpent in the wilderness, even so must the Son of Man be lifted up" (John 3:14). The devil is a serpent. If serpent means evil in this context, then we end up with some rather bad theology.

In the same way that a lion and a serpent do not always refer to Satan, leaven is not always a symbol of evil. A cake made with leaven was brought with the "peace offering for thanksgiving" in the Old Testament (Leviticus 7:13), and the wave offering was made with leavened loaves of bread, "as first fruits to the LORD" (Leviticus 23:17). The context should determine what the leaven is to symbolize. In Matthew 13:33, Jesus equates the kingdom of heaven with leaven, and there is nothing in this context to suggest that the leaven has an evil connotation since heaven is not evil. The text does not say that the kingdom of heaven will be corrupted like leaven. The kingdom of heaven is *like* leaven. The kingdom of heaven expands in the world like leaven expands when put in dough.

To make interpretive matters even worse, Pentecost tells us that the woman in the parable is a symbol "of a false religious system (Revelation 2:20; 17:1–8)."[20] Are women *always* symbols of evil? Jesus makes mention of women in a favorable way in other parables (Matthew 25:1–2; Luke 15:8). Why does Jesus mention a woman? As a description of evil? Hardly:

> It just so happens that women normally bake bread, as per the parable's demands (Leviticus 26:26; 1 Samuel 28:24), much like the three measures being an amount which would be fitting (Genesis 18:6; Judges 6:19; 1 Samuel 1:24). The woman *imports* the leaven *into* the meal, as Christ's kingdom comes from *without* (John 18:36; Revelation 21:2) and works *within* (Luke 17:20–21; Romans 14:17).[21]

There is no getting around it. God's kingdom is with us, and it will continue with us: "For the earth will be full of the knowledge of the LORD as the waters cover the sea" (Isaiah 11:9).

PART 5

THE CHRISTIAN AND THE FUTURE

"WE'RE LIVING
IN THE LAST DAYS"

David was not a believer in the theory that the
world will grow worse and worse, and that the
dispensations will wind up with general dark-
ness, and idolatry. Earth's sun is to go down
amid tenfold night if some of our prophetic
brethren are to be believed. Not so do we ex-
pect, but we look for a day when the dwellers
in all lands shall learn righteousness, shall trust
in the Saviour, shall worship thee alone, O
God, and shall glorify thy name. The modern
notion has greatly damped the zeal of the
church for missions, and the sooner it is shown
to be unscriptural the better for the cause of
God. It neither consorts with prophecy,
honours God, nor inspires the church with ard-
our. Far hence be it driven.

CHARLES H. SPURGEON

W hat do Barbara Streisand and Billy Graham have in common?
They both believe that the world is soon coming to an end.
Billy Graham writes:

> If you look in any direction, whether it is technological or physiological, the world as we know it is coming to an end. Scientists predict it, sociologists talk about it. Whether you go to the Soviet Union or anywhere in the world, they are talking about it. The world is living in a state of shock.[1]

There certainly is much truth in Dr. Graham's assessment of world conditions, but there is no biblical proof that we are living on the edge of history. As we will see, others have evaluated world conditions in their day and have come to a similar conclusion. These, too, have been wrong.

Predicting the end is not the sole domain of the Christian community. Barbara Streisand, singer and entertainer, has made a similar prediction. Her assessment is more of a gut feeling than any belief in the Bible's record of end-time events. She writes:

> I believe the world is coming to an end. I just feel that science, technology, and the mind have surpassed the soul—the heart. There is no balance in terms of feeling and love for fellow man.[2]

The small and the great, the sane and the insane, the sacred and the profane have been quick to predict when the end might come. They all have one thing in common: They have always been wrong! Each and every generation seems to have put together the details of what they believe to be end-time predictions to assure the world that they know that the end is near. Thus far the prophetic prognosticators have been wrong.

Some, desperate to know what the future holds, but refusing to believe that the Bible presents an accurate record of future events, are turning to Michel de Notredame, better known as Nostradamus (1503–1566), who supposedly envisioned the Great Fire of London (1666) and the rises of Napoleon Bonaparte and Adolf Hitler. His predictions are questionable, to say the least.[3] But it does show that predicting the end is not the sole property of the Christian community.

Destined to Repeat Itself

Unfortunately, few people seem to have learned any lessons from the failures of previous prophetic speculators. How many more will be lured into believing that the end is near as they read in Quatrain 10–72 of Nostradamus's prediction of the rise of "a great King of Terror" (the

> **"The small and the great, the sane and the insane, the sacred and the profane have been quick to predict when the end might come. They all have one thing in common: They have always been wrong!"**

Antichrist?) in July of 1999? What new world crisis will bring on the newest set of predictions? Only time will tell.

Crying Wolf

While predictions of the end abound in the unbelieving world, their failures only work to weaken the faith of those who believe in their already disintegrating worldview. There is a lesson in this for the Christian community. Some claim that there is little wrong with predicting the end since many people have been saved when they were told that all the signs are in place for Jesus to return in judgment. Over time, however, such assured predictions of the end have the effect of weakening the church's witness and work in the world. By "crying wolf" and being wrong each time, the church is perceived as unreliable. We might hear a critic of Christianity reason like this:

> If these self-proclaimed prophets were wrong on the timing of Jesus' return when they seemed so certain (particularly the rapture and the seven-year tribulation), then maybe they are wrong on other issues where they teach with equal certainty.

In addition, if one is positive that there is not much time left before the world falls apart, then why spend time fixing what is destined to break? Or, as some have put it, why polish brass on a sinking ship? For many modern-day prophets, it is April 14th, 1912—*Titanic* Earth has hit an iceberg, and she's sinking fast.

Prophetic Déjà Vu

As early as the second century, prophets were suggesting dates for the second coming of Christ. The prophet Montanus in A.D. 156 was one of the first to suggest a date for the Second Coming. His failed attempts at predicting the end did not deter other date setters.

> In the third century, a prophet called Novatian gathered a huge following by crying, "Come, Lord Jesus!" Donatus, a fourth-century prophet, commanded attention when he stressed that only 144,000 people would be chosen by God. He found this magic figure in Revelation 14:1 (a verse which the Jehovah's Witnesses use to proclaim their own version of this heresy). Both Novatian and Donatus were branded as heretics by the church.[4]

As the last day of 999 approached, "the old basilica of St. Peter's at Rome was thronged with a mass of weeping and trembling worshipers awaiting the end of the world" believing that they were on the eve of the millennium.[5] Land, homes, and household goods were given to the poor as a final act of contrition to absolve the hopeless from sins of a lifetime. Some Europeans sold their goods to make the trip to Palestine to await the Second Coming. This mistaken application of biblical prophecy happened again in 1100, 1200, and 1245. Prophetic speculation continued. "In 1531, Melchoir Hofmann announced that the second coming would take place in the year 1533. . . . Nicholas Cusa held that the world would not last past 1734."[6]

The Disappointed

Predictions of the impending return of Jesus have been rampant in the United States. William Miller (1782–1849), a farmer from Vermont, became an ardent Bible student, using only the marginal notes of his Bible and Cruden's *Concordance*, and formulated a prophetical system that influenced tens of thousands of devotees. In 1831 Miller preached his first sermon and followed these with a series of messages on Daniel 7 and 8.

Miller's popularity increased, and so did opposition to his teachings. Miller finally set a date for Jesus' return: 1843. "He arrived at this date by interpreting Daniel's seventy weeks (i.e., 490 days) as meaning 490

> **"Ideas have consequences. . . . If you are certain that Jesus is going to return in a few years, then this belief will have an impact on how you view this world and what you do to effect long-term change."**

---

years, on the principle that a day means a year of time. From the 490 years he subtracted AD 33, the date of the crucifixion (on the premise that Christ's death marks the end of the seventy weeks or 490 year-days), leaving 457."[7] By subtracting this date from the twenty-three hundred days (years) of Daniel 8:14, he was left with 1843 as the date of the second coming. When his prediction failed, Miller concluded that his date for the crucifixion was incorrect. After adjusting the date of the crucifixion, he predicted that the Second Coming would be on October 22, 1844. Nearly fifty thousand persons (some estimates make it one hundred thousand) left their churches to await the predicted event. "During the final week Millerites closed their stores, abandoned their crops and animals, and resigned from their posts."[8] The failed prophecies led to the "Great Disappointment," "when the movement collapsed, splintering into three main factions."[9] A similar "Great Disappointment" may meet the church if more failed predictions of the end greet an already skeptical world.

Ideas have consequences. Eschatological ideas can have long lasting consequences. If every generation believes as the Millerites did, then what is to become of this world? Should it be abandoned to evil? Should we throw in the towel and await the Second Coming in passivity? If you are certain that Jesus is going to return in a few years, then this belief will have an impact on how you view this world and what you do to effect long-term change. Some millennial adherents "found it difficult to adjust to the general enthusiasm for reform" in the nineteenth century "since it ran counter to the basic pessimism of their" end-time views.[10] For the most part, this idea prevails as we near the twenty-first century.

The Last Days

A lot of confusion exists over what the Bible means by the "last days." At least three views have been offered: (1) a concentrated period of time just prior to Jesus' Second Coming, making the time yet future; (2) the period of time between Jesus' first coming and Second Coming—typically and erroneously called the "church age"; (3) the forty-year period from a point in time just prior to Jesus' death, resurrection, and ascension to the destruction of Jerusalem in A.D. 70, which the Bible describes as a generation (forty years).

Which is the biblical view? The first view finds little support in Scripture since the writer to the Hebrews says:

> God, after He spoke long ago to the fathers in the prophets in many portions and in many ways, *in these last days* has spoke to us in His Son, whom He appointed heir of all things, through whom also He made the world. (Hebrews 1:1–2)

It is obvious from this passage and others like it that the last days were operating in the first century. This immediately dismisses the futuristic view which concentrates the last days as a period of time just before Jesus returns. We are left with views 2 and 3. While position 2 has its adherents, position 3 seems to make more sense, since to extend the last days over two thousand years seems a bit extreme. The Apostle Paul tells the Corinthians that the ends of the ages have come upon them: "Now these things happened to [Israel] as an example, and they were written for our instruction, *upon whom the ends of the ages have come*" (1 Corinthians 10:11, emphasis added).

The New Testament told its first readers that the "end of all things" was at hand, that is, the end of the Old Covenant with its types and

---

"It is obvious . . . that the last days were operating in the first century."

---

shadows was about to pass away. These events were to happen "soon"— soon to those who first read the prophecies. There is no getting around this language. Forcing these verses to describe a period nearly two thousand years in the future is "Scripture twisting":

- *"The night is almost gone, and the day is at hand.* Let us therefore lay aside the deeds of darkness and put on the armor of light." (Romans 13:12, emphasis added)
- "For the form of this world *is passing away.*" (1 Corinthians 7:31, emphasis added)
- "Let your forbearing spirit be known to all men. *The Lord is near.*" (Philippians 4:5, emphasis added)
- *"The end of all things is at hand;* therefore, be of sound judgment and sober spirit for the purpose of prayer." (1 Peter 4:7, emphasis added)
- "You too be patient; strengthen your hearts, *for the coming of the Lord is at hand.* Do not complain, brethren, against one another, that you yourselves may not be judged; behold, *the Judge is standing right at the door.*" (James 5:8–9, emphasis added)
- "Children, *it is the last hour;* and just as you heard that antichrist is coming, even now many antichrists have arisen; from this *we know that it is the last hour.*" (1 John 2:18, emphasis added)
- "The Revelation of Jesus Christ, which God gave Him to show to His bond-servants, *the things which must shortly take place.*" (Revelation 1:1, emphasis added)
- "And he said to me, 'These words are faithful and true'; and the Lord, the God of the spirits of the prophets, sent His angel to show

to His bond-servants *the things which must shortly take place.*" (Revelation 22:6, emphasis added)

- "And behold, *I am coming quickly.* Blessed is he who heeds the words of the prophecy of this book." (Revelation 22:7, emphasis added)
- "And he said to me, 'Do not seal up the words of the prophecy of this book, *for the time is near.*'" (Revelation 22:10, emphasis added)
- "Behold, *I am coming quickly,* and My reward is with Me, to render to every man according to what he has done." (Revelation 22:12; Matthew 16:27, emphasis added)
- "He who testifies to these things says, 'Yes, *I am coming quickly.*' Amen. Come, Lord Jesus." (Revelation 22:20, emphasis added)

These passages tell us that a significant event would occur in the lifetime of those who heard and read the prophecies. The last days were the final days of the Old Covenant order with its blood sacrifices, physical temple, and human priesthood. Jesus was the better and once-for-all sacrifice (Hebrews 9:11–22; 10:10–18); His body became the new and everlasting temple (John 2:19; Hebrews 9:11–12); He was a better priest "after the order of Melchizedek" (Hebrews 7). It was the new Covenant in His *own* blood (Luke 22:20).

Prophetic Provincialism

Contemporary Christians often hold to a provincial view of Bible interpretation. When Scripture mentions "wars and rumors of wars," for example, the assumption is that it must be referring to our era even though there have been "wars and rumors of wars" since Jesus uttered these memorable words nearly two thousand years ago. Our generation must be the rapture generation since world events point to the last days. Is it at least possible that Jesus was speaking of a period just before the destruction of Jerusalem where false Christs abounded, earthquakes shook the Mediterranean world, and famines decimated populations?[11] Could the church be misapplying these prophetic passages to the wrong era and, thus, be missing out on God's real plan for planet Earth?

Modern-Day Date Setters

The Millerite madness is still with us, although it has been reformulated and repackaged for popular consumption. In 1970 a book hit the bookstores that shook the Christian publishing industry. It was described as "the bestselling non-fiction book of the decade, selling more than 18 million copies worldwide." Since 1970, "more than 25 million copies have been printed in 30 languages."[12] The book is nearing its 110th printing.[13] The book? Hal Lindsey's *The Late Great Planet Earth*.

What made *The Late Great Planet Earth* so successful? First, it was written in a popular style, much like a work of fiction. Second, it got into the prediction game, interpreting current events in the light of Bible prophecy with an air of certainty. Third, it took a crystal ball approach to interpretation by giving its readers a sense of being able to gaze into the future. In fact, the final chapter in *The Late Great Planet Earth* is "Polishing the Crystal Ball."

There is a predictive keystone to Lindsey's prophetic edifice that, if pulled, brings the entire building crashing down on the precariously constructed system. What is the keystone?: Israel's rebirth as a nation in 1948. Without this keystone, the predictive elements in Lindsey's prophetic blueprint are nothing more than scattered bricks on an unorganized building site. If the rebirth of Israel is the keystone, then identifying the "generation of the fig tree" in Matthew 24:32 is the foundation stone of Lindsey's last-days structure.

> The most important sign in Matthew has to be the restoration of the Jews to the land in the rebirth of Israel. Even the figure of speech "fig tree" has been a historic symbol of national Israel. When the Jewish people, after nearly 2,000 years of exile, under relentless persecution, became a nation again on 14 May 1948 the "fig tree" put forth its first leaves.
>
> Jesus said that this would indicate that He was "at the door," ready to return. Then He said, "Truly I say to you, *this generation* will not pass away until all these things take place" (Matthew 24:34, NASB).
>
> What generation? Obviously, in context, the generation that would see the signs—chief among them the rebirth of Israel. A generation in the Bible is something like forty years. If this is a correct deduction, then within forty years or so of 1948, all these things could take place.

Many scholars who have studied Bible prophecy all their lives believe that this is so.[14]

The fig tree may be a *historic* figure for Israel (Lindsey does not show this to be true), but he has not shown it to be a *biblical* figure. Contrary to Lindsey, "the context of Jesus' words in Matthew 24:32–33 gives no warrant to the idea that Jesus was using the figure of the fig tree as anything more than an illustration on how the Jews were able to tell when summer was near."[15] In fact, it is the olive tree that is the *biblical* figure for Israel (Romans 11:17–24)). In addition, Luke's gospel does not seem to see anything unique in the fig tree illustration since he tells us to "behold the fig tree, *and all the trees*"(Luke 21:29, emphasis added). If the fig tree represents Israel, then according to Matthew 21:19, "No longer shall there ever be any fruit from" Israel. It has withered and died (21:20). Lindsey is wrong about the fig tree being a sign of "the restoration of the Jews to the land in the rebirth of Israel." There is nothing in Matthew 24, Mark 13, or Luke 21 that describes such an event. This view must be read into the texts.

What significance does "this generation" have in Lindsey's scenario? For Lindsey, "a generation is something like forty years." By adding forty years to 1948 we get 1988. But Lindsey is a *pretribulationist*.[16] He believes that the rapture occurs seven years *before* Jesus returns to set up His millennial kingdom. This means that the rapture should have occurred, using Lindsey's timetable, sometime around 1981 with 1988 being the year of the Second Coming and the establishment of the earthly millennial reign.

Just in case Lindsey's prediction proved to be wrong, he covered himself with phrases like "*if* this is a correct deduction," "*something like* forty years," "forty years *or so*," and "*could* take place." Lindsey's prophetic guesses, however, were not considered guesses by his readers. Many took the rebirth of Israel and the forty-year generation scenario as date setting. Many set their sights on the almost assured imminent return of Christ.

A Clouded Crystal Ball

Gary Wilburn, in his review of the film-version of *The Late Great Planet Earth*, seems to agree that the 1948–1988 scenario is the keystone to

Lindsey's multimillion best seller. "The world," according to Lindsey, "must end within one generation from the birth of the State of Israel. Any opinion of world affairs that does not dovetail with this prophecy is dismissed."[17] Lindsey in his *The 1980s: Countdown to Armageddon,* while still hedging, leads his readers to a pre-1990 climax of history: "I believe many people will be shocked by what is happening right now and what will happen in the very near future. *The decade of the 1980s*

"The church has not learned from the failed predictions of end-time speculators."

---

could very well be the last decade of history as we know it."[18] Well, we are in the 1990s. The rapture did not occur as Lindsey said it would, based on the 1948–1988 timetable and a forty-year generation.

And neither did the Jupiter Effect. The "Jupiter Effect" was to have been an astronomical "situation in which all of the planets of our solar system become aligned in a straight line perpendicular to the sun. This alignment causes great storms on the sun's surface, which in turn affect each of the planets" resulting in a "tremendous strain on the Earth's faults, touching off earthquakes."[19]

> According to our author-experts, some of the scary side-effects of the new wave of quakes will be great floods—when dams built over faults are destroyed—and nuclear power plant meltdowns at facilities built on or near the Earth's faults.[20]

The Jupiter effect had no effect. This was just another in a whole series of failed predictions by Hal Lindsey that added to the credibility gap that exists in the church.

In addition, there were to be changes in weather patterns and lower food production that were to have resulted in "hunger and misery of millions" that "would provoke a great global holocaust."[21] Again, failed predictions.

Hero or Bum?

While Lindsey did not assure his readers that we would not see the '90s, his intimations have led many Christians to believe that the end was quite near:

> In an interview published in *Christianity Today* in April 1977, Ward Gasque asked Lindsey, "But what if you're wrong?" Lindsey replied: "Well, there's just a split second's difference between a hero and a bum. I didn't ask to be a hero, but I guess I have become one in the Christian community. So I accept it. But if I'm wrong about this, I guess I'll become a bum."[22]

Lindsey has since revised his thinking on the length of a generation. In 1977 Lindsey wrote: "I don't know how long a biblical generation is. Perhaps somewhere between sixty and eighty years."[23] In an article entitled "The Eschatology of Hal Lindsey," published in 1975, Dale Moody wrote: "If the 'Great Snatch,' as Lindsey repeatedly calls the Rapture, does take place before the Tribulation and by 1981, I will beg forgiveness from Lindsey for doubting his infallibility as we meet in the air."[24] It is Lindsey who needs to apologize.

The church has not learned from the failed predictions of end-time speculators. Many prophetic wizards have gone before us, and as history will attest, they have been wrong about the near demise of planet Earth. The list of end-time prognosticators is endless, from Montanus in A.D. 156 to Edgar C. Whisenant in 1988 (and again in 1989).[25] As world conditions deteriorate, do not be surprised if new predictions are forthcoming. The same Bible verses have been lined up generation after generation to "prove" that we are living in the last days.

A Sign of Hope?

Chuck Smith, pastor of Calvary Chapel in Costa Mesa, California, was convinced that the Lord would be coming for His church before the end of 1981. While he stated that he could be wrong, he nevertheless stated his beliefs with certainty: "It's a deep conviction in my heart, and all my plans are predicated upon that belief."[26] Chuck Smith's views on the timing of the Lord's return demonstrate the danger of setting dates. His plans were predicated on the almost certain return of Jesus. Since he wrote this in 1978, this would mean that his temporal plans would extend no longer than *three years!* Rebuilding takes time. But there is no time when

---

"We should be wary of allowing current events to shape the way we interpret Scripture."

---

the end is three years off. Since the Lord did not return in 1981, Chuck Smith now states: "Date setting is wrong, and I was guilty of coming close to that. I did believe that Hal Lindsey could have been on track when he talked about the forty-year generation, the fig tree budding being the rebirth of Israel, and I was convinced in my own heart."[27]

Now, it should be pointed out that just because people have been wrong in their suppositions about the end in the past does not mean, at least logically, that Jesus' return cannot be imminent. I'm only saying that we should be wary of allowing current events to shape the way we interpret Scripture. It's certainly possible that we are living on the edge of history (although there is no way of knowing), but as some scholars have pointed out, Jesus' return could be a thousand years off.[28] Think of the implications of that scenario! Your view of the future will affect the way you live in the present and the way you plan or fail to plan for tomorrow. A shortened time frame will lead you to abandon the future to the humanists as we are witnessing in our own day.

The Effects of Prediction

Some of the Thessalonian Christians were "leading an undisciplined life, doing no work at all, but acting like busybodies" (2 Thessalonians

3:11). While this may have little to do with a preoccupation with "the day of the Lord" (1 Thessalonians 5:2), it reminds us that God requires us to work regardless of external circumstances. Faithfulness is evaluated in terms of kingdom work: "Who then is the faithful and sensible slave whom his master put in charge of his household to give them their food at the proper time? Blessed is that slave whom his master finds so doing when he comes" (Matthew 24:45–46). Jesus goes on to hint at the time and circumstances of His coming: "The master of that slave will come on a day *when he does not expect him and at an hour which he does not know*" (24:50, emphasis added). Nowhere does Scripture intimate that we should cease any aspect of our work for the kingdom, even if we *think* Jesus' coming is near. *"The delay of the master made no difference to the true servant*: he busied himself about his Lord's business. . . . But the master's delay induced the false servant to a sinful course of action. *The Lord's delay brought out the true character of his servants*."[29]

Jesus related a parable to His disciples when "they supposed that the kingdom of God was going to appear immediately" (Luke 19:11). In Jesus' day many of His disciples assumed the kingdom would arrive through a cataclysmic event. Jesus told them through the parable to "do business . . . until I come back" (19:13). When the master finally returns he will take an accounting. Those who made a profit on the money given by the master will "be in authority over" ten and five cities (19:17–19). The one who put the money "away in a handkerchief" (19:20), not being industrious enough to put the money in the bank to collect interest (19:23), loses everything (19:24).

We have not seen the last of the prophetic speculators. The Christian has a duty to ignore their timetables but not to ignore the work to which we have all been called to do.

"IT'S NEVER RIGHT TO RESIST AUTHORITY"

In Germany they came for the Communists, and I didn't speak up because I wasn't a Communist. Then they came for the Jews, and I didn't speak up because I wasn't a Jew. Then they came for the trade unionists, and I didn't speak up because I wasn't a trade unionist. Then they came for the Catholics, and I didn't speak up because I was a Protestant. Then they came for me, and by that time no one was left to speak up.

PASTOR MARTIN NIEMÖLLER

In 1660 John Bunyan disobeyed the law of England by preaching without a license. He was arrested at a church meeting and put in prison so damp that he said it was enough to 'make the moss grow on one's eyebrows.' There he converted his prison into a pulpit and wrote the greatest of all Christian classics, *Pilgrim's Progress*. He was told that he would be released if he promised not to further violate the law for which he was imprisoned, but he refused to do so. He was arrested two more times for the same act of disobedience."[1] Bunyan was in good company. Peter and John were arrested "because they were teaching the people and proclaiming in Jesus the resurrection from the dead" (Acts

4:2). Even after their release, like Bunyan, they continued to preach the gospel, "for we cannot stop speaking what we have seen and heard" (4:20).

Why a chapter on resistance? First, there are many misconceptions about the topic. Some Christians conclude, based solely on their understanding of Romans 13 and Matthew 22:21, and without any consideration of other passages, that Christians are obligated to obey those in authority over them no matter what the command or circumstances. This is an untenable position, as a careful study of Scripture will demonstrate.

Second, as Christians make an impact on society, they can expect harsh treatment from those who have "no king but Caesar" (John 19:15). The early church certainly experienced the wrath of those who wanted to perpetuate the status quo. For example, at the preaching of the gospel, Jason and some brethren were dragged before the city authorities, with the following charge made against them: "These men [Paul and Silas] who have upset the world have come here also; and Jason has welcomed them, *and they all act contrary to the decrees of Caesar*, saying that there is another king, Jesus" (Acts 17:6–7, emphasis added; 4:12). The early Christians faced numerous challenges by angry citizens and powerful ecclesiastical and civil rulers. As the church at the end of the twentieth century begins to work out the implications of God's kingdom through the preaching of the gospel and the application of His Word to every facet of life, persecution will undoubtedly follow.

Third, without explicit biblical guidelines, resistance can lead to revolution. The Bible does not support either anarchy or revolution as ways to advance God's kingdom. The orthodox church has always been antirevolutionary but proresistance. The Christian's positive obedience to God is seen as disobedience to man (resistance). Therefore, the Christian is not purposefully resisting civil authority; he is simply following the stipulations of the greater covenant which have the effect of overruling the covenants of men.

> When Peter and the other apostles were arrested and imprisoned by the Sanhedrin for refusing to obey the order not to preach in the name of Jesus, their defense was, "We must obey God rather than men" (Acts 5:29; cf. 4:19). As F. F. Bruce has commented, the "au-

thority of the Sanhedrin was great, but greater still was the authority of Him who commissioned them to make this good news known."[2]

Fourth, time is on the side of Christians. The corrupt worldview of humanism cannot succeed. As it becomes more and more consistent with its self-contradictory ideology, it self-destructs. Through abortion,

---

"Some Christians conclude . . . that Christians are obligated to obey those in authority over them no matter what the command or circumstances. This is an untenable position."

---

homosexuality, and a contemptuous attitude toward the biblical family, the humanists are limiting their future. There is no need for revolution by Christians. Christians are instead to remain faithul in the midst of humanist self-destruction.

Sovereignty's Limitations

No human authority is absolute. In Matthew 22:21, Jesus tells the Pharisees and the Herodians to "render to Caesar the things that are Caesar's." He does not say, "render to Caesar everything Caesar commands." We are only to render those things that *are* Caesar's. This implies limitations. The things that are God's do not belong to Caesar. Is Jesus giving Caesar, and by analogy, all civil governments, unlimited authority to rule as they please without regard to God's commandments? Even Caesar is to render "to God the things that are God's." Moreover, we know from Romans 13:1 that the authority that Caesar has is given to him by God.

The Old Testament

There is no doubt that Christians are to submit "for the Lord's sake to every human institution, whether to a king as the one in authority, or to governors as sent by him for the punishment of evildoers and the praise of those who do right" (1 Peter 2:13–14). David showed by example how this principle should be followed. When given the opportunity to kill King Saul, David refused: "Behold, this day your eyes have seen that the LORD had given you today into my hand in the cave, and some said to kill you, but my eye had pity on you; and I said, 'I will not stretch out my hand against my lord, for he is the LORD's anointed'" (1 Samuel 24:10). Keep in mind that Saul was pursuing David to have him killed. David's example should be a lesson to Christians everywhere that resistance to duly constituted authority is a serious matter. A great deal of biblical support must be gathered before the decision to resist, that is, to obey God rather than man, is made. The Old Testament shows that resistance to tyranny was legitimate. David did resist Saul's pursuit of him, but he did not kill him when he had the opportunity. David was neither an anarchist nor a revolutionary.

The Hebrew Midwives

The Hebrew midwives were commanded by the king of Egypt to put to death all the male children being born to the Hebrew women (Exodus 1:15–16). The Hebrew midwives disobeyed the edict of the king: "But the midwives feared God, and did not do as the king of Egypt had commanded them, but let the boys live"(1:17). The midwives had to make a choice. Did God's law overrule the command of a king, even the king of Egypt? God shows His approval of their actions: "So God was good to the midwives, and the people multiplied, and became very mighty. And it came about because the midwives feared God, that He established households for them" (1:20–21).

In 1982 a juvenile court judge, the Honorable Randall J. Hekman, "in direct opposition to the law of the land, which said women cannot be denied an abortion," refused to grant permission for a pregnant thirteen-year-old to obtain an abortion. Was he wrong? His decision parallels that of the midwives who refused to follow the directive of the king of Egypt. In a letter to the editor of a Grand Rapids, Michigan, newspaper, Judge Hekman explained why he refused to grant the abortion to the thirteen-year-old:

> What if the law requires a judge to order the execution of a person known to be totally innocent? What if a judge is required by law to order Jewish people to concentration camps or gas chambers because the law says that Jews are non-persons? . . .
>
> Ten short years ago, a judge in Michigan would be guilty of a felony crime if he encouraged, much less ordered that a pregnant girl obtain an abortion. Then, in 1973, the Supreme Court ruled that all state laws making abortion a crime were unconstitutional. In one day, that which had been a reprehensible crime became a sacred right protected by the Constitution itself.[3]

"Hekman was severely criticized in the press and by judicial colleagues. The child is now in grade school and is presumably more supportive of the judge's decision!"[4]

"There is no need for revolution by Christians. Christians are instead to remain faithul in the midst of humanist self-destruction."

Jochebed's Deception

Jochebed, Moses' mother, also disobeyed the edict of the king by hiding her child and later creating a way of escape for him so he would not be murdered by the king's army: "But when she could hide him no longer, she got him a wicker basket and covered it over with tar and pitch. Then she put the child into it, and set it among the reeds by the bank of the Nile" (Exodus 2:3). Jochebed even deceived Pharaoh's daughter into believing that she, Jochebed, was in no way related to the child (2:7–9).

During the Nazi Holocaust, Jews were hidden from the Nazis. This was a crime against the state. Was it wrong? In terms of Nazi law, yes. In terms of the Bible, no. The ten Boom family, best known through Corrie ten Boom and her book *The Hiding Place*, risked their lives to save Jews who were being hunted down by representatives of the German government. Under biblical law, their actions were legitimate.

Of Lying and Spies

Rahab hid the spies of Israel and lied about their whereabouts. When a route for escape became available, she led them out another way from that of the pursuing soldiers. The king issued a command to Rahab: "Bring out the men who have come to you, who have entered your house, for they have come to search out all the land" (Joshua 2:3). She disobeyed a direct command of the king of Jericho. Some want to maintain that Rahab was right in "welcom[ing] the spies in peace" (Hebrews 11:31), but she was wrong in lying about the whereabouts of the spies. The following is a representative example:

> We see, therefore, that neither Scripture itself nor the theological inferences derived from Scripture provide us with any warrant for the vindication of Rahab's untruth and this instance, consequently, does not support the position that under certain circumstances we may justifiably utter an untruth.[5]

This is nonsense. Welcoming the spies in peace when they came in, and then answering truthfully that they were still in her house when the officials questioned her, are contradictory practices. "Welcom[ing] them in peace" means that they would not fall in the hands of the king of Jericho which would have meant certain death. Rahab had changed her allegiance from Jericho to Israel. Conditions of war were operating. If she had told the truth to the men seeking the two spies, then she would have been an accomplice in their deaths (cf. Psalm 50:18).

There is another point that is often missed in this story about Rahab's lie. "Joshua the son of Nun sent two men as *spies secretly* from Shittim. . . (Joshua 2:1, emphasis added). The text continues by telling us that "they went and came into the house of a harlot whose name was Rahab, and lodged there." Did they announce that they were Israelite spies? Joshua says the operation was to be done "secretly," that is, without revealing the truth of their mission. Are not spies in the business of lying? Why was Joshua right to send men to spy out the land, while Rahab was wrong to lie about the route the spies took? Why were the spies right to hide? Is not that an act of deception? Why didn't they rebuke Rahab for lying? Why didn't the spies leave by the same route they entered the city? Instead, they were accomplices in Rahab's lie by allowing her to "let them down by a rope through the window" (2:15).

Rahab is praised by two New Testament writers for her actions: "By faith Rahab the harlot did not perish along with those who were disobedient, after she had welcomed the spies in peace" (Hebrews 11:31). Rahab is listed with Abraham as one whose faith was reflected in her works: "And in the same way [as Abraham] was not Rahab the harlot also justified by works, when she received the messengers and sent them out by another way?" (James 2:25). By sending the spies out by another way, she subverted the king's desire to capture the spies. God commended Rahab for deception. Again, the circumstances were atypical. "The critics of Rahab's lie apparently think her case is analogous to David's adultery with Bathsheba, a union which ultimately produced Solomon. We are not, of course, bound to praise David's action simply because Solomon's rule produced many desirable results (such as the construction of God's temple). We are *specifically told* that David's adultery was abhorrent in the eyes of God; we are *not* so informed about Rahab's actions."[6]

When you go out at night, do you keep a light on in the house? Some people go so far as to purchase a device that turns lights on and off at random intervals to give the appearance that people are at home. This is done to mislead burglars. Isn't this deception? Are you not lying?

Are resistance movements during times of war biblical? How about clandestine operations? Should we abolish the C.I.A. and counterintelligence agencies? Is it wrong to mask messages by sending them in code? Is it proper to wear camouflage? Would it be wrong to send false messages to the enemy to lead them in a direction that would hinder their ability to attack? Truth-telling "does not apply to acts of war. Spying is legitimate, as are deceptive tactics in warfare. Protection from thieves requires concealment and walls."[7]

The Rescue of Jonathan

Jonathan nearly met with a certain death because of his father's decree that any man who ate food before evening, before the king had avenged himself of his enemies, would be cursed (1 Samuel 14:24). Jonathan had unknowingly violated the law. The leaders, when called by Saul to be questioned as to who violated the law, remained silent. When King Saul learned that it was his own son, he was determined to enforce his edict by punishing Jonathan with death: "And Saul said, 'May God do this to me and more also, for you shall surely die, Jonathan'" (14:44). The people confronted the king: "'As the LORD lives, there shall not one hair of his head fall to the ground, for he has worked with God this day.' So the people rescued (literally, ransomed) Jonathan and he did not die" (14:45).

Saying No to a King

Shadrach, Meshach, and Abed-nego refused to follow the command of the king to worship the golden statue: "These men, O king, have disregarded you; they do not serve your gods or worship the golden image you have set up" (Daniel 3:12). When the three were thrown into the furnace, the angel of the Lord came to their aid (3:25). This shows that there are consequences in opposing an edict of a ruler. Some have suffered martyrdom because of their refusal to obey. "In the year A.D. 165 Justin Martyr and his companions refused to yield to the command of the emperor and sacrifice to the pagan gods. 'Do what you will. For we are Christians and offer no sacrifice to idols.' Justin and his companions were beheaded for their faithfulness to the Savior."[8]

King Darius signed a document that prohibited anyone from making "a petition to any god or man besides" himself (Daniel 6:7). Anyone refusing to obey the order "shall be cast into the lion's den" (6:7). Daniel refused to heed the edict's restrictions. The Bible states that Daniel went out of his way to disobey the order: "Now when Daniel knew that the document was signed, he entered his house (now in his roof chamber he had windows open toward Jerusalem); and he continued kneeling on his knees three times a day, praying and giving thanks before his God, as he had been doing previously" (6:10).

The New Testament

The New Testament has similar accounts of resistance to tyranny. When Peter and John were ordered by the rulers and elders of the people to stop preaching in the name of Jesus (Acts 4:18), the two apostles refused to follow their injunction: "Whether it is right in the sight of God to give heed to you rather than to God, you be the judge; for we cannot stop speaking what we have seen and heard" (4:19–20). Peter and John could not stop speaking what they had seen and heard because they had been commanded by Jesus to preach in His name (Matthew 28:18–20; Acts 1:8; 1 Corinthians 9:16).

"Either God or man is sovereign. When these sovereignties clash and conflict, the Christian, first a citizen of heaven, must obey God rather than men."

On another occasion, some of the apostles were arrested for preaching and healing in the name of Jesus. Again, they were put in a public jail (Acts 5:18). During the night "an angel of the Lord . . . opened the gates of the prison" and commanded them to disobey the rulers of Israel: "Go your way, stand and speak to the people in the temple the whole message of this Life" (5:20). When the apostles again were confronted with the command not to preach and teach, their response was quick and sure: "We must obey God rather than men" (5:29).

The apostles' obedience to God conflicted with the desires of the state. This resulted in the first apostolic death by the hands of a civil authority: "Now about that time Herod the king [Agrippa I] laid hands on some who belonged to the church, in order to mistreat them. And he had James the brother of John put to death" (Acts 12:1–2). Peter was later arrested for similar crimes against the state (12:3). Obeying

God rather than men is legitimate. God certainly set the example when He sent one of His angels to release Peter from prison (12:6–8).

Either God or man is sovereign. When these sovereignties clash and conflict, the Christian, first a citizen of heaven, must obey God rather than men. "William Tyndale (1490) taught that the truths of Scripture had authority over both the state and the church. Partly for this 'heresy,' government authorities in England tried to capture him, but Tyndale evaded them for years. He was finally caught, tried as a heretic, and executed in 1536."[9]

What About Revolution?

None of the above examples should lead the Christian to assert that God has called the individual Christian to anarchy or the church to promote revolution in the name of some "sacred cause." America's Revolutionary War was neither anarchistic nor revolutionary in the modern sense. The thirteen colonies were operating civil governments, having a contractual relationship with the King of England. The king violated the terms of the agreement. The disputants were independent civil governments, not individuals or mobs. The war for independence "was not a lawless rebellion against authority, as some historians claim. Rather, it was a *legal interposition* of one lawfully elected level of government (the colonial legislatures) against a king who insisted in obdurately breaking his feudal contract with the colonies."[10] This understanding of our nation's constitutional beginnings has been lost on the modern mind:

> For years we have been taught that we are the product of a revolutionary generation who, because of religious, economic, and political disagreements, finally (through anarchistic and violent means) tore themselves from a loving and legally constituted government.[11]

Too often Americans are quick to support every revolutionary uprising around the world because of the good result of America's revolution. They fail to recognize that our revolution was different in character and kind.

As the above authors demonstrate, the modern view of America's revolution is "at variance with the actions and beliefs of those who participated in the 'Revolution.'. . . . The American colonists did not revolt against constitutional authority; they did not seek independence from the King of England. The king, instead, severed all ties with his

---

"Since individuals and churches are not given the sword, they cannot legitimately revolt against the existing civil powers. But legitimate civil governments can."

American colonies. The Declaration of Independence was not written to gain independence but to maintain and define what had been forced upon the colonies."[12]

> The Declaration's purpose was to inform a "candid world" that an action of the King and Parliament had cast the thirteen colonies out of the British Empire. The document did not proclaim legal, formal severance from England; that had already been accomplished by George III and Parliament on Friday, December 22, 1775.[13]

The colonies wanted a dissolution only of the "political bands." The colonists and their governments had kept their part of the contract with the Crown. Therefore, any discussion of the legitimacy or illegitimacy of the colonists' actions is best handled under the topic of war. While revolutions are generated by "the people" *against* existing civil governments, wars are fought by one existing government against another existing civil government. The people are conscripted by the opposing civil governments to defend their national sovereignty. The colonies were civil governments with their own constitutions and governors. Some Christian writers fail to understand the dynamics behind the colonies' war with England. The following is a representative example:

> It is understandable that everyone would like to believe that the revolution in his country was just, even if those in other countries are not.

But in all honesty, given the biblical criteria listed here, it is not possible to justify the American Revolution either.[14]

None of the "biblical criteria" that this author sets forth in his book fit the circumstances surrounding the American revolution. In his chapter on war, the author summarizes his position by stating that "God has ordained government and given it the sword."[15] The thirteen colonies were sovereign civil governments that had been given the sword. They had their own courts and judges. Since individuals and churches are not given the sword, they cannot legitimately revolt against the existing civil powers. But legitimate civil governments can.

Romans 13

Because of its no-exception tone, Romans 13 is seen as prohibiting all resistance to the law of the state: "Let every person be in subjection to the governing authorities" (13:1). The apostle lists no exceptions. Peter makes a similar statement: "Submit yourselves for the Lord's sake to every human institution, whether to a king as the one in authority, or to governors as sent by him for the punishment of evildoers and the praise of those who do right" (1 Peter 2:13–14). Again, no exceptions. Now, this is the same Peter who declared, "We must obey God rather than men" (Acts 5:29; 4:19–20). How do we reconcile the apparent contradiction?

There are a number of places in Scripture where one verse speaks in absolute terms and another verse offers an exception. This is not unusual. If I tell my children to go outside and play until dinner is ready, I have spoken in absolute terms. They are not to come into the house until they are called. No exceptions are given. What if it rains? What if a large dog enters the yard? Can they enter the house without violating my absolute and no-exception command? They would not be violating my no-exception command because there are *unspoken* exceptions. They are assumed to be operating without them having to be repeated each time a new command is given. They have been told on previous occasions to "come in when it's raining" and "do not get near stray dogs that wander into the yard."

The Bible operates in the same manner. In one place Jesus says, "All those who take up the sword shall perish by the sword" (Matthew 26:52). Does this include the civil magistrate? What about the person who strikes an assailant in self-defense? Is this not an exception to Jesus' no-exception statement? Since the Bible already discusses self-defense (Exodus 21:23–25; Leviticus 24:19–21; Deuteronomy 19:21) and the role of the civil magistrate (Genesis 9:6), there is no need to repeat the exceptions since His hearers know that Jesus has anarchy and revolution in mind (Leviticus 19:18), not the just use of the sword. Romans 13:4 informs us that it is the duty of the civil magistrate to use the sword. Is this a contradiction? No.

So then, when we read passages like Romans 13:1 and 1 Peter 2:13–14, we must not neglect the rest of the Bible that is equally authoritative and more fully explains these passages.

> Many general statements of Scripture must be open to admitting exceptions even though qualifications are not immediately spelled out. Why are so many generalizations stated without qualification? *Because the exact conditions restricting their applicability are not known, or because the "accidental" or providential circumstances that render them inapplicable occur so seldom as to be practically negligible, or because such a qualification has already been stipulated in another inscripturated context.*[16]

In summary, we must recognize that as the state becomes more tyrannical and non-Christian in its social and political policies, conflicts between church and state will multiply. Those conflicts may make it necessary for Christians to say no to statist laws that will force them to violate the laws of God. There is an additional reason why Christians must understand the limits of civil jurisdiction *and* the limits of resistance. Because of a desire to see the current corruption in our own nation reversed, some Christians may take it upon themselves to bring about change by revolutionary means. This is an unbiblical agenda to pursue. There is no warrant in Scripture for a revolutionary spirit.

CONCLUSION

It makes a big difference that the Ten Com-
mandments are found in the Supreme Court
building instead of selections from the code of
Hammurabi and that our coins say "In God
We Trust" instead of "In Baal We Trust."
It makes a big difference that the Library of
Congress has a quotation from a Psalm, in-
stead of a quotation from the Koran.

PETER J. LEITHART AND GEORGE GRANT

The Word of God has been replaced by the word of man. Ours is a day of "Bible-phobia," even among Christians; the Bible is a religious book that only has a word for private morality, and only if a person *chooses* to follow its precepts. The Bible, we are told, does not speak to the world. Those evangelicals who contend that it does speak to the world assure us that it speaks solely in general terms. There is no *specific* word.

While the Bible may be believed in principle, it is too often denied in practice. When we are told that "Christians must address 'issues' in the society," the following disclaimer is often given: "but not institutions." How does one address issues but not institutions since "issues arise within institutions and cannot be properly addressed unless one has some idea of what an institution in God's world should be like"?[1] The key to fighting any evil is to understand how God's world works. Without that understanding there is no possibility of changing anything. There must be a model. That model must come from the person who designed the model. God has designed the world, and the Bible is the owner's manual on how it works. "Without a model, we draw our options over issues from the alternatives presented by the society."[2] This is exactly what the church has done. Prevailing anti-Christian ideologies have shaped the church's view of the world. The world has become the measuring stick for change, all in the name of the notion that "the Bible cannot be used as a standard for cultural change." The following quotation is a representative example:

> The Christian life is life in the Holy Spirit, not life governed by detailed regulations as was the life of God's people in Old Testament times. The New Testament does contain a few rules (e.g., "Pay just wages"; "pay your taxes"), but the believer under the authority of Scripture is spiritually liberated to keep the moral law in good conscience in a diversity of cultural contexts and political structures.[3]

This approach leaves the Christian with few regulations. "A diversity of cultural contexts and political structures" mitigates against the application of a narrowly focused law, even if it's from God. The absence of specific biblical regulations means an ethical free-for-all. If the Christian's life is not regulated by "detailed regulations," then we can't expect much from the Bible to be applied to the world at large.

We have moved from specific guidelines to being "moved by the Holy Spirit." The Spirit and the Word are never in opposition. Much has been done in the name of the Holy Spirit, and not all of it can be supported by Scripture. But what does it mean, for example, to pay your taxes? Is the state free to tax citizens at any rate? Are there biblical norms for taxation? If there are no detailed regulations, then the state is free to confiscate all our income by an appeal to the *general* law "pay your taxes." Keep in mind that the prohibition regarding abortion is found with those laws that Dr. Carl Henry says are no longer obligatory during the New Testament era (Exodus 21:22–25).[4] There is no direct prohibition of abortion in the New Testament, although it is certainly possible to infer such a prohibition (Luke 1:41), but only because the Old Testament is more specific. Neither will you find a prohibition of bestiality in the New Testament (Exodus 22:19; Leviticus 18:23–25).

The Stepchild of the Enlightenment

Western culture is no longer seen as the child of the Reformation but an heir of the Enlightenment.[5] Of course, in one sense Western culture is now Enlightenment culture, and abortion is evidence that the refor-mational worldview has been discarded. The question is: Should our

---

"While the Bible may be believed in principle, it is too often denied in practice."

---

nation follow the path laid down by the Enlightenment philosophers, or should we work to recover the worldview of the Reformation?

> The utopian dream of the Enlightenment can be summed up by five words: reason, nature, happiness, progress, and liberty. It was thor-oughly secular in its thinking. The humanistic elements which had risen during the Renaissance came to flood tide in the Enlightenment. Here was man starting from himself absolutely. And if the humanistic elements of the Renaissance stand in sharp contrast to the Reforma-tion, the Enlightenment was in total antithesis to it. The two stood for and were based upon absolutely different things in an absolute way, and they produced absolutely different results.[6]

Cotton Mather wrote a history of early New England which he ti-tled *Magnalia Christi Americana*, or *The Great Achievement of Christ in America*. "The sum of the matter," he explained, "is that from the be-ginning of the Reformation in the English nation, there had always been a generation of godly men, desirous to pursue the reformation of religion, according to the Word of God." But in England, there were others with "power. . . in their hands" who desired "not only to stop the progress of the desired reformation but also, with innumerable vexation, to persecute those that most heartily wish well unto it." These early Christian settlers were "driven to seek a place for the exercise of the Protestant religion, according to the light of conscience, in the deserts of America." Their purpose was nothing less than to complete the Ref-ormation, believing "that the first reformers never intended that what they did should be the absolute boundary of reformation."[7]

The Reformation, while still influencing many in the church, has taken a back seat to the Enlightenment worldview that spawned the French Revolution, Darwinism, Marxism, National Socialism, and the present abortion industry. The spirit of the French Declaration of the Rights of Man (August 26, 1789), where "'the Supreme Being' equaled 'the sovereignty of the nation'—that is, the general will of the people,"[8] has usurped the reformational and biblical view that sovereignty is God's alone, and He delegates a limited amount of sovereignty to individuals and institutions (e.g., family, church, and state). Whether it's "we the people," the French "citizen," the Nazi *Volk,* or the Marxist "proletariat," man rules, and in such a world the lives of the weakest and most despised are always in jeopardy.

Modern man's ideological tool for change is evolution. Harold O. J. Brown writes that "our present 'abortion revolution' is possible only on the basis of the widespread replacement of our perception of ourselves as rational creatures made in the image of God, with the perception of ourselves as mere accidental by-products of what Jacques Monod calls 'chance and necessity,'—in other words, with the general triumph of social Darwinism."[9]

What nature used to do by chance, man now initiates by terroristic design. The evolutionary doctrine of the "survival of the fittest" has been commandeered by modern man for the betterment of society. A calculated show of force by the mother, her doctor, and the autonomous courts is used to eliminate the defenseless unborn for high social reasons.

After a debate on the abortion issue, a pro-life lawyer who had taken part had the opportunity to speak with some of the participants.

> Most of the students *already* recognized that the unborn child is a human life. Nevertheless, certain social reasons are considered "high enough" to justify ending that life. According to some of the women, examples of "high enough" reasons include protecting pregnant teenagers from the psychological distress of bearing a child, helping poor women who aren't able to care adequately for a child, and preventing children from coming into the world "unwanted." Many charged that pro-life philosophies are not "socially acceptable" because they fail to deal realistically with these problems.[10]

Abortion is simply state-sanctioned Darwinism. The state reflects the views of those who vote for the prevailing leadership.[11] "If man has no individual dignity, no immortal soul, no destiny outside political

---

> **"The key to fighting any evil is to understand how God's world works. . . . God has designed the world, and the Bible is the owner's manual on how it works."**

---

order, then abortion—like fornication, adultery, and sodomy—becomes a trivial matter."[12] There are enough people who have made their voices heard; they want abortion, no matter that it means taking a human life. "High social reasons" have become the moral touchstone for the nation.

NOTES

Introduction

1. For a more complete study of this topic, see Gary DeMar, "Goodbye, Columbus?" *The Biblical Worldview* (September 1990). In addition to the flat-earth myth, few people are aware that Columbus was a Christian who wanted to take the gospel to the lost around the world. See August J. Kling, "Columbus—A Layman 'Christ-bearer' to Unchartered Isles," *The Presbyterian Layman* (October 1971), 4. Columbus set forth his ideas in his *Libro de las Profecias* or *Book of Prophecies* which he had in hand when he appealed to Queen Isabella for funds to make his voyage. Large portions of the *Book of Prophecies* have been translated. See Kay Brigham, *Christopher Columbus: His Life and Discovery in the Light of His Prophecies* (Barcelona, Spain: Clie, 1990). While the comments of the author lean heavily toward dispensational premillennialism, the translation of the Scripture passages that Columbus chose to support his views is very helpful. The most intriguing aspect of Columbus's *Book of Prophecies* is his belief that the gospel of the kingdom still had to be preached to all the nations before Jesus would come again.

2. Samuel Eliot Morison, *Admiral of the Ocean Sea: A Life of Christopher Columbus* (Boston, MA: Little, Brown and Co., 1942), 89.

3. Richard Shenkman, *Legends, Lies, and Cherished Myths of American History* (New York: William Morrow, 1988), 13.

4. Samuel Eliot Morison, *The European Discovery of America: The Northern Voyages* (New York: Oxford University Press, 1971), 6.

5. Morison, *Admiral of the Sea*, 89.

6. Sam Dargan, "Will the Real Christopher Columbus Please Stand Up?" *World* (October 7, 1989), 20.

7. Morison, *The European Discovery of America*, 7.

8. False. The ark rested on the "mountains [plural] of Ararat."

9. These words are not found in the Bible (cf. Genesis 3:19; 18:27; Job 30:19). They are found in the *Book of Common Prayer* and are often used at burial services to remind us of our creaturely beginnings, that we are but dust (Psalm 103:14).

10. Not quite. The setting for the crucifixion is identified in all four Gospels as a place outside the city called "The Skull." "Luke also calls the execution site 'The Skull' (Greek *kranion*), which appears in the Latin Vulgate Bible as 'the place of the

skull' (*calvariae locus*). When the Latin Bible was translated into English (Rheims, 1582), the Latin wording was retained as a proper name, 'Calvary.' The KJV retained the Rheims translation, but all modern English translations use the English 'skull.'" David C. Downing, *What You Know Might Not Be So: 220 Misrepresentations of Bible Texts Explained* (Grand Rapids, MI: Baker Book House, 1987), 34.

11. Nearly every manger scene has three wise men visiting Jesus along with the shepherds. First, the Bible does not tell us how many wise men came, only that "magi from the east arrived in Jerusalem" (Matthew 2:1). The fact that three gifts are mentioned may have led some to believe that only three magi were present (2:11). The Christmas hymn "We Three Kings of Orient Are" has added to the confusion. Second, by the time the magi found Jesus, He was in a "house" (2:11). Third, since Herod had children who were two years old and younger killed, one might conclude that Jesus was not a newborn.

12. D. A. Carson, *The Sermon on the Mount: An Exegetical Exposition of Matthew 5–7* (Grand Rapids, MI: Baker Book House, 1978), 39–40.

13. Larry Poston, "The Adult Gospel," *Christianity Today* (August 20, 1990), 25.

Chapter 1: "The World Is Evil"

1. Gary T. Amos, *Defending the Declaration: How the Bible and Christianity Influenced the Writing of the Declaration of Independence* (Brentwood, TN: Wolgemuth and Hyatt, 1989), 105–06.

2. Arthur F. Holmes, *Contours of a World View* (Grand Rapids, MI: Eerdmans, 1983), 57.

3. Robert E. Webber, *Common Roots: A Call to Evangelical Maturity* (Grand Rapids, MI: Zondervan, 1978), 205.

4. John Pearson, *An Exposition of the Creed*, 2 vols., 3rd ed. (Oxford, England: Oxford University Press, 1847), 1:79.

5. John Eyre Yonge, *An Exposition of the Apostles' Creed* (London: Hodder and Stoughton, 1887), 27.

6. R. K. Harrison, *The Wycliffe Exegetical Commentary: Numbers* (Chicago, IL: Moody Press, 1990), 279.

7. Robert Browning (1812–1889), *Pippa Passes*, Part I, 1.222.

8. Bishop Joseph Henshaw (1603–1679), *Horae Succisivae* (1631), Part I.

9. Abraham Lincoln (1809–1865), *Address at Dedication of National Cemetery at Gettysburg* (Nov. 19, 1863).

10. Thomas Paine (1737–1809), *The Rights of Man* (1792), Part II, Chapter 5.

11. A. E. Housman (1859–1936), *Last Poems* (1922), "Lancer," 12.

12. The World Series involves only two nations—the United States and Canada—and yet, it's still called the "World Series."

13. William Shakespeare (1564–1616), *The Tragedy of Othello the Moor of Venice* (1604), Act I, Scene 3, 156.

14. B. C. Johanson, "The Definition of 'Pure Religion' in James 1:27 Reconsidered," *Expository Times* 84 (1973), 118–19. Quoted in Peter Davids, *Commentary on James*, New International Greek Testament Commentary (Grand Rapids, MI: Eerdmans, 1982), 103.

15. Greg L. Bahnsen, "The Person, Work, and Present Status of Satan," *The Journal of Christian Reconstruction*, Symposium on Satanism, ed. Gary North I:2 (Winter 1974), 23–24.

16. Os Guinness, *The Dust of Death: A Critique of the Establishment and the Counter Culture—and a Proposal for a Third Way* (Downers Grove, IL: InterVarsity Press, 1973), 5.

17. Albert M. Wolters, *Creation Regained: Biblical Basics for a Reformational Worldview* (Grand Rapids, MI: Eerdmans, 1985), 54.

Chapter 2: "Involvement in the World Is Not 'Spiritual' "

1. S. M. Houghton, *Sketches from Church History: An Illustrated Account of 20 Centuries of Christ's Power* (Carlisle, PA: The Banner of Truth Trust, 1980), 28.

2. Ibid.

3. David Chilton, *Paradise Restored: A Biblical Theology of Dominion* (Ft. Worth, TX: Dominion Press, 1985), 3–4.

4. Philip E. Hughes, *Commentary on the Second Epistle to the Corinthians*, NICNT (Grand Rapids, MI: Eerdmans, 1962), 256.

5. Guinness, *The Gravedigger File*, 78.

6. Greg L. Bahnsen, "This World and the Kingdom of God," in Gary DeMar and Peter Leithart, eds. *The Reduction of Christianity: A Biblical Response to Dave Hunt* (Ft. Worth, TX: Dominion Press, 1988), 351.

7. From the Greek word *to seem*.

8. P. Richard Flinn, "Baptism, Redemptive History, and Eschatology: The Parameters of Debate," in James B. Jordan, ed. *Christianity and Civilization: The Failure of the American Baptist Culture* 1 (Spring 1982), 144–45.

9. Murray J. Harris, *From Grave to Glory: Resurrection in the New Testament* (Grand Rapids, MI: Zondervan, 1990), 402.

10. Glenn Tinder, "Can We Be Good Without God?" *The Atlantic Monthly* (December 1989), 69.

11. Ibid.

12. Joseph Spradley, "A Christian View of the Physical World," in Arthur Holmes, ed. *The Making of a Christian Mind: A Christian World View and the Academic Enterprise* (Downers Grove, IL: InterVarsity Press, 1985), 68.

13. Herbert Schlossberg, *Idols for Destruction: Christian Faith and Its Confrontation with American Society* (New York: Regnery/Gateway, [1983] 1990), 273.

Chapter 3: "The Bible Is Only Concerned About Salvation"

1. Edward E. Plowman, ed., *National and International Religion Report* (July 2, 1990), 4.

2. Charles Colson, "The Kingdom of God and Human Kingdoms," in *Transforming Our World: A Call to Action* (Portland, OR: Multnomah, 1988), 154–55.

3. Rousas J. Rushdoony, *The Institutes of Biblical Law* (Phillipsburg, NJ: Presbyterian and Reformed, 1973), 113; 449.

4. Noel Weeks, *The Sufficiency of Scripture* (Carlisle, PA: The Banner of Truth Trust, 1988), 252.

5. Joseph Spradley, "A Christian View of the Physical World," in Arthur Holmes, ed. *The Making of a Christian Mind: A Christian World View and the Academic Enterprise* (Downers Grove, IL: InterVarsity Press, 1985), 60.

6. Douglas Groothuis, "Revolutionizing Our Worldview," *The Reformed Journal* (November, 1982), 23.

7. Larry Burkett, *What the Bible Says About Money* (Brentwood, TN: Wolgemuth and Hyatt, 1989).

8. Gary DeMar, *Ruler of the Nations: Biblical Principles for Government* (Ft. Worth, TX: Dominion Press, 1987).

9. For a comprehensive discussion of many of these topics see Gary DeMar, *God and Government*, 3 vols. (Brentwood, TN: Wolgemuth and Hyatt, 1990).

Chapter 4: "You Cannot Legislate Morality"

1. Archie P. Jones, "Christianity and the First Amendment: The Truth About the Religion Clauses of the Constitution," unpublished manuscript, 3.

2. R. C. Sproul, "Creating Justice," *Eternity* (November 1986), 19.

3. Rousas J. Rushdoony, *Law and Liberty* (Tyler, TX: Thoburn Press, [1971] 1977), 1–2.

4. See Gary DeMar, "Homosexuality: An Illegitimate Alternative Deathstyle," *The Biblical Worldview* 3 (1) (January 1987), 1–4.

5. J. H. Bavinck, *An Introduction to the Science of Missions* (Nutley, NJ: Presbyterian and Reformed, 1960), 12–13.

6. R. C. Sproul, *Abortion: A Rational Look at an Emotional Issue* (Colorado Springs, CO: NavPress, 1990), 90–91.

7. For a discussion of multiple governmental roles, see Gary DeMar, *God and Government: A Biblical and Historical Study* (Brentwood, TN: Wolgemuth and Hyatt, [1982] 1990).

Chapter 5: "Christians Should Remain Neutral"

1. "Neutrality Carries the Day," *Christianity Today* (September 10, 1990), 74.

2. Rheta Grimsley Johnson, "'People' vs. Fundamentalists," *The Marietta Daily Journal* (September 2, 1986), 4A.

3. Joan Connell, "American Children are Becoming Moral Illiterates," *Marietta Daily Journal* (October 11, 1990), 5B.

4. Ibid.

5. Ibid.

6. Ibid.

7. Charles Colson, "From a Moral Majority to a Persecuted Minority," *Christianity Today* (May 14, 1990), 80.

8. Harvey Cox, *The Secular City* (New York: Macmillan, 1965). Quoted in Franky Schaeffer, *A Time for Anger: The Myth of Neutrality* (Westchester, IL: Crossway Books, 1982), 24.

9. A radio editorial heard on WGST, Atlanta, GA (September 12, 1986).

10. William L. Shirer, *The Rise and Fall of the Third Reich* (New York: Simon and Schuster, 1960), 236. Emphasis added.

11. E. L. Hebden Taylor, "Religious Neutrality in Politics," *Applied Christianity* (April 1974), 19.

12. Doug Bandow, *Beyond Good Intentions: A Biblical View of Politics* (Westchester, IL: Crossway Books, 1988), 16.

13. Ibid., 76.

Chapter 6: "Jesus Was Not a Social Reformer"

1. Noel C. Burtenshaw, "Imitation of Jesus Not Mere Celibacy," *The Atlanta Journal/Constitution* (August 26, 1990), C-2.

2. Otto Zöckler, "Saint Francis of Assisi and the Franciscan Order," in Samuel Macauley Jackson, ed. *The New Schaff-Herzog Encyclopedia of Religious Knowledge*, 15 vols. (Grand Rapids, MI: Baker Book House, 1952), 4:359.

3. "The Rule of Francis," in Tim Dowley, ed. *Eerdmans' Handbook to the History of Christianity* (Grand Rapids, MI: Eerdmans, 1977), 266–267.

4. For a discussion of this difficult passage, see Gordon D. Fee, *The First Epistle to the Corinthians*, NICNT (Grand Rapids, MI: Eerdmans, 1987), 277–80.

5. Mikhail Khorev, *Letters from a Soviet Prison Camp* (Grand Rapids, MI: Baker Book House, 1989).

6. "Concerning Religious Societies," Resolution of the Central Committee, 8 April 1929, para. 17. Cited in Evgeny Barabanov, "The Schism Between the Church and

the World," in Alexander Solzhenitsyn, ed. *From Under the Rubble* (Boston: Little, Brown and Company, 1975), 180.

7. Donald G. Bloesch, *Crumbling Foundations: Death and Rebirth in an Age of Upheaval* (Grand Rapids, MI: Zondervan, 1984), 30.

8. Barbara Reynolds, "Religion Is Greatest Story Ever Missed," *USA Today* (March 16, 1990), 13A.

9. Ibid.

10. Merrill C. Tenney, *New Testament Times* (Grand Rapids, MI: Eerdmans, 1965), 152.

11. Ethelbert Stauffer, *Christ and the Caesars*, K. and R. Gregor Smith, trans. (Philadelphia, PA: The Westminster Press, 1955), 140.

12. Madsen Pirie, *The Book of the Fallacy* (London: Routledge and Kegan Paul, 1985), 19.

13. Kenneth L. Gentry, Jr., *Before Jerusalem Fell: Dating the Book of Revelation* (Tyler, TX: Institute for Christian Economics, 1989), 193–219.

14. John Baillie, *The Belief in Progress* (New York: Charles Scribner's Sons, 1951), 199.

15. Larry Poston, "The Adult Gospel," *Christianity Today* (August 20, 1990), 25.

16. George W. Lasher, "Regeneration—Conversion—Reformation," in R. A. Torrey, A. C. Dixon, et al., eds., *The Fundamentals: A Testimony to the Truth*, 4 vols. (Grand Rapids, MI: Baker Book House, [1917] 1988), 3:140.

17. James B. Jordan, *Through New Eyes: Developing a Biblical View of the World* (Brentwood, TN: Wolgemuth and Hyatt, 1988), 267.

Chapter 7: "The Church Should Not Be Involved in Social Issues"

1. John Wingate Thornton, *The Pulpit of the American Revolution or, The Political Sermons of the Period of 1776 with a Historical Introduction, Notes, and Illustrations* (New York: Burt Franklin, [1860] 1970), xxxviii. Emphasis in original.

2. Cited in ibid., xxiii. Emphasis in original.

3. Ibid., xxii–xxiii. Emphasis in original.

4. Ibid., xxv.

5. O. Palmer Robertson, "Reflections on New Testament Testimony Concerning Civil Disobedience," *Journal of the Evangelical Theological Society* 33(3) (September 1990), 332.

6. Charles David Eldridge, *Christianity's Contributions to Civilization* (Nashville, TN: Cokesbury Press, 1928), 21.

7. Ibid.

8. William Hendriksen, *Exposition of Colossians and Philemon* (Grand Rapids, MI: Baker Book House, 1964), 233.

9. Gary North, *Tools of Dominion: The Case Laws of Exodus* (Tyler, TX: Institute for Christian Economics, 1990), 111–206; 209–47, and James B. Jordan, *The Law of the Covenant: An Exposition of Exodus 21–23* (Tyler, TX: Institute for Christian Economics, 1984), 75–92.

10. North, *Tools of Dominion*, 125.

11. Eldridge, *Christianity's Contributions to Civilization*, 25.

12. Ibid., 26–28.

13. John D. Woodbridge, Mark A. Knoll, and Nathan O. Hatch, *The Gospel in America: Themes in the Story of America's Evangelicals* (Grand Rapids, MI: Zondervan, 1979), 233.

14. Ibid.

15. Ibid., 234.

16. John Pollock, *Wilberforce* (Belleville, MI: Lion Publishing, [1977] 1986), 51.

17. Quoted in Charles Colson, *Kingdoms in Conflict* (Grand Rapids, MI: Zondervan, 1987), 100.

18. Ibid., 104.

19. Otto J. Scott, *The Secret Six: John Brown and the Abolitionist Movement* (New York: Times Books, 1979), 85.

20. Lester B. Scherer, *Slavery and the Churches in Early America, 1619–1817* (Grand Rapids, MI: Eerdmans, 1975), 39.

21. John Stott, *Involvement: Being a Responsible Christian in a Non-Christian Society* (Old Tappan, NJ: Revell, 1984), 20.

22. Quoted in Gabriel Sivan, *The Bible and Civilization* (New York: Quadrangle/The New York Times Book Co., 1973), 77.

23. For a history and theology of caring for the poor, see George Grant, *Bringing in the Sheaves: Transforming Poverty into Productivity* (Brentwood, TN: Wolgemuth and Hyatt, [1985] 1988).

24. Quoted in Sivan, *The Bible and Civilization*, 77.

25. "Medicine's Religious Roots," *Christianity Today* (September 10, 1990), 34.

26. Gordon W. Jones, "Introduction" to Cotton Mather, *The Angel of Bethesda: An Essay Upon the Common Maladies of Mankind* (Barre, MA: American Antiquarian Society, [1724] 1972), xv.

27. Robert H. Bremner, *American Philanthropy* (Chicago: University of Chicago Press, [1960] 1982), 12.

28. Eldridge, *Christianity's Contributions to Civilization*, 33.

29. Ibid., 34.

30. Jonathan Mayhew, *A Discourse Concerning Unlimited Submission and Non-Resistance to the Higher Powers*, January 30, 1750 in Thornton, *The Pulpit of the American Revolution* (Boston: Gould and Lincoln, 1860), 47-48.

31. Norris Magnuson, *Salvation in the Slums: Evangelical Social Work, 1865–1920* (Grand Rapids, MI: Baker Book House, [1977] 1990), xiii.

32. Stott, *Involvement*, 23.

33. Finney, quoted from "Letters on Revivals—No. 23," *The Oberlin Evangelist* (n.d.) in Donald Dayton, *Discovering an Evangelical Heritage* (Peabody, MA: Hendrickson Publishers, [1976] 1988), 20. Dayton writes that "Letters on Revivals—No. 23" is left out of modern editions of these letters. He calls it an "egregious example of censorship" (p. 19).

Chapter 8: "Politics Is Dirty"

1. Quoted in Robert Duncan Culver, *Toward a Biblical View of Civil Government* (Chicago: Moody Press, 1974), 72.

2. Robert L. Thoburn, *The Christian and Politics* (Tyler, TX: Thoburn Press, 1985), 17.

3. John Eidsmoe, *God and Caesar: Christian Faith and Political Action* (Westchester, IL: Crossway Books, 1984), 56.

4. Daniel R. Grant, *The Christian and Politics* (Nashville, TN: Broadman Press, 1968), 12.

5. Paul Johnson, *The Enemies of Society* (New York: Atheneum, 1977), 117.

6. Joel Belz, "Evidence Mounts: We Are Still a Small Minority," *World* (October 13, 1990), 3.

7. Cited in Frederick Nymeyer, "Neighborly Love and Ricardo's Law of Association," *First Principles in Morality and Economics* (South Holland, IL: Libertarian Press, 1958), 31.

8. J. Howe, "The Changing Political Thought of John Adams." Quoted in Wayne House, ed., *Restoring the Constitution: 1787–1987* (Dallas, TX: Probe Books, 1987), 10.

9. George Bancroft, *History of the United States from the Discovery of the American Continent*, 10 vols. (Boston: Little, Brown and Company, 1860), 8:442.

10. Quoted in Loraine Boettner, *The Reformed Doctrine of Predestination* (Nutley, NJ: Presbyterian and Reformed, [1932] 1969), 383.

11. John T. McNeill, *The History and Character of Calvinism* (New York: Oxford University Press, 1954), 348.

12. M. E. Bradford, *A Worthy Company* (Westchester, IL: Crossway Books, 1988), viii.

Chapter 9: "Religion and Politics Do Not Mix"

1. *Reynolds v. Ruggles* (1811), cited in Edwin S. Gaustad, *Faith of Our Fathers: Religion and the New Nation* (New York: Harper and Row, 1987), 117.

2. Gary DeMar, *God and Government: A Biblical and Historical Study* (Brentwood, TN: Wolgemuth and Hyatt, 1990), 3–31; 198–204; and *Ruler of the Nations: Biblical Principles for Civil Government* (Ft. Worth, TX: Dominion Press, 1987).

3. Herbert Schlossberg, *Idols for Destruction: Christian Faith and Its Confrontation with American Society* (New York: Regnery/Gateway, [1983] 1990), 6.

4. Quoted in Erik von Kuehnelt-Leddihn, *Leftism: From de Sade and Marx to Hitler and Marcuse* (New Rochelle, NY: Arlington House, 1974), 313.

5. Joseph M. Stowell, *The Dawn's Early Light: Daring to Challenge the Deepening Darkness* (Chicago: Moody Press, 1990), 52–53.

6. Ibid., 53.

7. Cited in John Eidsmoe, *The Christian Legal Advisor* (Grand Rapids, MI: Baker Book House, [1984] 1987), 150.

8. Ibid.

9. Benjamin Hart, *Faith and Freedom: The Christian Roots of American Liberty* (Dallas, TX: Lewis and Stanley Publishers, 1988), 357.

10. Quoted in William Dannemeyer, *Shadow in the Land: Homosexuality in America* (San Francisco, CA: Ignatius Press, 1989), 57.

11. *National and International Religion Report* (October 22, 1990), 5.

12. "Georgia Judge Overturns Death Sentence Because Jury Consulted Bible," *ALL News: The Official Newsletter of the Pro-Life Movement* (April 7, 1989), 7. As the following case demonstrates, the Bible has been brought into a Georgia court:

    > Iron pins are a common and useful means of identifying property corners and they and other similar monuments serve a useful purpose. The installation and maintenance of permanent monuments identifying land corners even preserves the good order of society itself. From earliest times the law not only authorized but protected landmarks. Interference with landmarks of another was a violation of the Mosaic law. See Deuteronomy 19:14; 27:17; Job 24:2; Proverbs 22:28; 23:10. (256 Ga. 54, *International Paper Realty Company v. Bethune*. No. 43092. Supreme Court of Georgia, June 10, 1986).

13. *Church of the Holy Trinity v. The United States* (143 United States 457), 1892.

14. *Chronicles* (November 1989), 7–8.

15. *New York Times* (January 12, 1981).

16. "'God' Removed from Notaries' Oath," *The Kansas City Star* (February 18, 1990), 2A.

17. "Judges Prayer Banned," *Marietta Daily Journal* (October 20, 1990), 4A.

18. There is nothing unconstitutional about a judge uttering a prayer in a courtroom. The Bible is still used in many courts to swear in witnesses, with the witnesses acknowledging with "So help me God." Congressional chaplains are constitutional: "The legislature by majority vote invites a clergyman to give a prayer; neither the inviting nor the giving nor the hearing of the prayer is making a law. On this basis alone . . . the saying of prayers, per se, in the legislative halls at the opening session is not prohibited by the First and Fourteenth Amendments" (*Chambers v. Marsh*, 463 U.S. 783 [1982], 675 F. 2d 228).

19. Under the Federal Judiciary Act of 1789, no witness could testify who "did not believe that there is a God who rewards truth and avenges falsehood." This requirement was not changed until 1906. The general consensus of the time held that an atheist could not be trusted as a witness: "The Court of Common Pleas of Chester County (New York) . . . rejected a witness who declared his disbelief in the existence of God. The presiding judge remarked, that he had not before been aware that there was a man living who did not believe in the existence of God; that this belief constituted the sanction of all testimony in a court of justice; and that he knew of no cause in a Christian country where a witness had been permitted to testify without such belief." The New York *Spectator* (August 23, 1831), quoted in Alexis de Tocqueville, *Democracy in America*, 2 vols. (New York: Alfred A. Knopf, [1834, 1840] 1960), 1:306.

20. Leo Pfeffer, *Church, State, and Freedom* (Boston: The Beacon Press, 1953), 9.

21. Ibid., 9–10.

22. Ibid., 10.

23. Ibid.

24. Schlossberg, *Idols for Destruction*, 185.

25. Pfeffer, *Church, State, and Freedom*, 11.

26. Francis A. Schaeffer, *How Should We Then Live?* in *The Complete Works of Francis A. Schaeffer: A Christian Worldview*, 5 vols. (Westchester, IL: Crossway Books, 1982), 5:149.

27. Henry M. Morris, *The Long War Against God: The History and Impact of the Creation/Evolution Conflict* (Grand Rapids, MI: Baker Book House, 1989), 311.

28. Schlossberg, *Idols for Destruction*, 178.

29. These quotations by Hegel can be found in Karl R. Popper, *The Open Society and Its Enemies*, 2 vols., 4th ed. (Princeton, NJ: Princeton University Press, 1963), 2:31.

30. Schlossberg, *Idols for Destruction*, 185.

31. Henry Mayr-Harting, "The West: The Age of Conversion (700–1050)," in John McManners, ed. *The Oxford Illustrated History of Christianity*, (New York: Oxford University Press, 1990), 101.

32. Kuyper, *Lectures on Calvinism*, 78.

33. Mayr-Harting, "The West: The Age of Conversion (700–1050)," 102.

34. Kenneth Gentry, "The Greatness of the Great Commission," in Gary North, ed. *The Journal of Christian Reconstruction*, Symposium on Evangelism, 3(2) (Winter 1981), 45.

Chapter 10: "The Christian's Citizenship Is in Heaven"

1. Quoted in Charles Colson, *Kingdoms in Conflict* (Grand Rapids, MI: Zondervan, 1987), 140.

2. William L. Shirer, *The Nightmare Years: 1930–1940* (Boston: Little, Brown and Company, 1984), 152.

3. Ibid.

4. Ibid., 153.

5. A quotation of Hitler's confirmed by Hermann Rauschning, once a confidant of Hitler, in Rauschning's book *The Voice of Destruction* (New York: G. P. Putnam's Sons, 1940), 297–300. Quoted in ibid., 152.

6. William L. Shirer, *The Rise and Fall of the Third Reich* (New York: Simon and Schuster, 1960), 236.

7. Quoted in Shirer, *The Nightmare Years*, 154.

8. Fustel de Coulanges, *The Ancient City: A Study on the Religion, Laws, and Institutions of Greece and Rome* (Garden City, NY: Doubleday Anchor [1864] 1955), 196. Quoted in Gary North, *Political Polytheism: The Myth of Pluralism* (Institute for Christian Economics, 1989), 62.

9. Shirer, *Rise and Fall of the Third Reich*, 200.

10. Karl Marx and Friedrich Engels, *The Communist Manifesto*, 1848.

11. John Howard Yoder, *The Politics of Jesus* (Grand Rapids, MI: Eerdmans, 1972), 195.

12. Robert Duncan Culver, *Toward a Biblical View of Civil Government* (Chicago: Moody Press, 1974), 49–50.

13. Jacques Ellul, *The Subversion of Christianity*, *The Subversion of Power* (Grand Rapids, MI: Eerdmans, 1986), 115.

14. The Greek word in this passage is "age." But there are other New Testament passages where Satan is described as being "the ruler of the world" (John 14:30). "Age" and "world" seem to be used synonymously.

15. R. B. Kuiper, "The Word of God Versus the Totalitarian State," *Westminster Theological Journal* XI (November 1948). Quoted in Gary North, ed., *The Journal of Christian Reconstruction*, Symposium on Politics 5(1) (Summer 1978), 170.

16. William Hendriksen, *Exposition of the Gospel According to John*, New Testament Commentary, 2 vols. (Grand Rapids, MI: Baker Book House, 1953–54), Vol. 2, 60.

17. Philip E. Hughes, *Commentary on the Second Epistle of the Corinthians*, The New International Commentary on the New Testament (Grand Rapids, MI: Eerdmans, 1962), 127.

18. Greg L. Bahnsen, "The Person, Work, and Present Status of Satan," Gary North, ed. *The Journal of Christian Reconstruction*, Symposium on Satanism, 1(2) (Winter, 1974), 22.

19. Martin Luther, "A Mighty Fortress is Our God," third verse.

20. Quoted in Hughes, *Commentary on Second Corinthians*, 128.

Chapter 11: "God's Kingdom Has Not Come"

1. This view of the kingdom is advocated by dispensational premillennialists. Dispensationalism asserts that Jesus offered to Israel a physical, political, earthly kingdom, but that the Jews rejected Jesus as their king, thus initiating the kingdom's "postponement." Such a view contradicts Scripture. First, Scripture nowhere states this. Second, Scripture tells a different story: "Jesus therefore perceiving that they were intending to come and take Him by force, to make Him king, withdrew again to the mountain by Himself alone" (John 6:15). It was the idea of a political kingdom that Jesus rejected, the same type of kingdom that dispensationalists say is yet to be established.

2. Greg L. Bahnsen and Kenneth L. Gentry, Jr., *House Divided: The Break-Up of Dispensational Theology* (Tyler, TX: Institute for Christian Economics, 1989), 181.

3. Ibid., 186.

4. Albert M. Wolters, *Creation Regained: Biblical Basics for a Reformational Worldview* (Grand Rapids, MI: Eerdmans, 1985), 65.

5. Gary North, *Unconditional Surrender: God's Program for Victory*, 2nd ed. (Tyler, TX: Institute for Christian Economics, 1983), 126.

6. Note that the gospels say that both "the kingdom of heaven" and "the kingdom of God" are near. The phrase, "kingdom of heaven," appears only in Matthew. There is, however, no sharp distinction between these two terms. Whatever distinctive shade of meaning Matthew might have given to "heaven," he uses the two phrases to refer to the same thing. See especially Matthew 19:23–24, where Jesus tells His disciples that it is hard for a rich man to enter the kingdom of heaven (19:23), and that it is easier for a camel to go through the eye of a needle than for a rich man to enter the kingdom of God (19:24). Clearly, the two phrases are parallel and, for all practical purposes, synonymous. For a discussion of this, see Oswald T. Allis, *Prophecy and the Church* (Philadelphia: Presbyterian and Reformed, 1945), 299ff.

7. Hermann Ridderbos, *The Coming of the Kingdom* (Philadelphia: Presbyterian and Reformed, 1962), 48.

8. George Eldon Ladd, *Jesus and the Kingdom: The Eschatology of Biblical Realism*, 2nd ed. (Waco, TX: Word, 1964), 107.

9. George Eldon Ladd, *A Theology of the New Testament* (Grand Rapids, MI: Eerdmans, 1974), 65–66. See 2 Corinthians 10:14, where the same verb is used.

10. A. A. Hodge, *Evangelical Theology* (Edinburgh: Banner of Truth, [1890] 1976), 227.

Chapter 12: "There Is a Separation Between Church and State"

1. Nancy Leigh DeMoss, ed., *The Rebirth of America* (Philadelphia, PA: The Arthur S. DeMoss Foundation, 1986), 87.

2. Public Law 97—280, 96 Stat. 1211, approved October 4, 1982.

3. For an opposing view, see Gary North, *Political Polytheism: The Myth of Pluralism* (Tyler, TX: Institute for Christian Economics, 1990).

4. John Howard Yoder, *The Politics of Jesus: Vicit Agnus Noster* (Grand Rapids, MI: Eerdmans, 1972), 42.

5. Kay Withers, "Religion Will Return to Poland's Classrooms," *St. Petersburg Times* (September 16, 1990), 25 and 26A.

6. Quoted by Judge Brevard Hand, in *Jaffree v. Board of School Commissioners of Mobile County*, 544 F. Supp. 1104 (S. D. Ala. 1983) in Russell Kirk, ed., *The Assault on Religion: Commentaries on the Decline of Religious Liberty* (Lanham, NY: University Press of America, 1986), 84.

7. Hand, *Jaffree v. Board of School Commissioners*, 22–23.

8. Benjamin Weiss, *God in American History: A Documentation of America's Religious Heritage* (Grand Rapids, MI: Zondervan, 1966), 153–205.

9. Peter J. Ferrara, *Religion and the Constitution: A Reinterpretation* (Washington, DC: Free Congress Foundation, 1983), 34–35.

10. Leo Pfeffer, *Church, State and Freedom* (Boston: Beacon Press, 1953), 98.

11. Ferrara, *Religion and the Constitution*, 36.

12. From a letter to John Adams, October 12, 1813.

13. Ernest Campbell Mossner, "Deism," *The Encyclopedia of Philosophy*, ed. Paul Edwards, 8 vols. (New York: Macmillan, 1967), 2:334.

14. Norman L. Geisler, *Is Man the Measure?* (Grand Rapids, MI: Baker Book House, 1983), 124–25.

15. John Adams to Thomas Jefferson, June 28, 1813, in Lester J. Cappon, ed., *The Adams-Jefferson Letters*, 2 vols. (Chapel Hill, NC: University of North Carolina Press, 1959), 2:339–40. Quoted in Gary T. Amos, *Defending the Declaration: How the Bible and Christianity Influenced the Writing of the Declaration of Independence* (Brentwood, TN: Wolgemuth and Hyatt, 1989), 9.

16. Ibid.

17. "The Treaty of Tripoli," *The Rutherford Institute* 2(1) (January/February 1985), 10.

18. Cited in Charles Bevans, *Treaties and Other International Agreements of the United States of America 1776–1959*, Vol. 11 (Washington, DC: Department of State, 1974), 1070.

19. All citations from treaties can be found in William M. Malloy, compiler, *Treaties, Conventions, International Acts, Protocols and Agreements Between the United States of America and Other Powers*, 4 vols. (New York: Greenwood Press [1910], 1968).

Chapter 13: "God's Kingdom Is Not of This World"

1. John Eliot, *The Christian Commonwealth: or, The Civil Policy of the Rising Kingdom of Jesus Christ* (1659). Quoted in John Eidsmoe, *Christianity and the Constitution: The Faith of Our Founding Fathers* (Grand Rapids, MI: Baker Book House, 1987), 23–34.

2. Quoted in Martha Lou Lemmon Stohlman, *John Witherspoon: Parson, Politician, Patriot* (Louisville, KY: Westminster/John Knox Press, 1976), 114.

3. From a taped interview with Peter Lalonde and Dave Hunt, "Dominion and the Cross," Tape #2 of *Dominion: The Word and New World Order*, distributed by the *Omega-Letter*, Ontario, Canada, 1987. Emphasis added. There is a similar quotation in Dave Hunt, *Beyond Seduction: A Return to Biblical Christianity* (Eugene, OR: Harvest House, 1987), 250.

4. In a letter to me (January 16, 1988), Hunt writes to clarify his position: "It is true that you have found a quote or two in which I was careless with my language." In this same letter, Hunt states that the future earthly millennium is "the temporary earthly manifestation of God's kingdom promised to Israel that becomes the final proof of the incorrigible nature of the human heart."

5. Dave Hunt, *Whatever Happened to Heaven?* (Eugene, OR: Harvest House, 1988), 255.

6. Dave Hunt and T. A. McMahon, *The Seduction of Christianity* (Eugene, OR: Harvest House, 1985), 224.

7. David Wilkerson, "The Laodicean Lie!" (Lindale, TX: World Challenge), 4.

8. William F. Arndt and F. Wilbur Gingrich, *A Greek-English Lexicon of the New Testament and Other Early Christian Literature* (Chicago: University of Chicago Press, 1957), 233–236. This lexicon, the standard dictionary of New Testament Greek, has a two-and-one-half page discussion, in small print, of the various meanings of the two-letter preposition, *ek*.

9. F. Godet, *Commentary on the Gospel of John*, Timothy Dwight, trans. 2 vols. (New York: Funk and Wagnalls, 1886), 2:369.

10. R. C. H. Lenski, *The Interpretation of St. John's Gospel* (Minneapolis, MN: Augsburg, [1943] 1961), 1229.

11. B. F. Westcott, *The Gospel According to St. John*, (Grand Rapids, MI: Eerdmans, 1958), 260.

12. Quoted by John Lofton, "Our Man in Washington," Number 18, December 1986. (Vallecito, Ca.: Chalcedon Foundation).

13. Robert Duncan Culver, *Toward a Biblical View of Civil Government* (Chicago, IL: Moody, 1974), 195.

14. R. V. G. Tasker, *The Gospel According to John* (Grand Rapids, MI: Eerdmans, 1960), 201.

15. J. Dwight Pentecost, *Things to Come* (Grand Rapids, MI: Zondervan, 1958), 146. Emphasis added. A similar view can be found in *The New Scofield Reference Bible* (New York: Oxford University Press, 1967), 1015.

16. Kenneth L. Gentry, Jr., "Dispensational Dyslexia," *Dispensationalism in Transition* (October 1990), 1.

17. Pentecost, *Things to Come*, 147.

18. Pentecost, *Things to Come*, 148.

19. Richard Chenevix Trench, *Notes on the Parables of Our Lord*, 14th ed. (London: Macmillan and Co., 1882), 117.

20. Ibid.

21. Gentry, "Dispensational Dyslexia," 2.

Chapter 14: "We're Living in the Last Days"

1. Quoted in Mike Evans, *The Return* (Nashville, TN: Thomas Nelson, 1986), 22.

2. Ibid., 222

3. James Randi, *The Mask of Nostradamus: A Biography of the World's Most Famous Prophet* (New York: Charles Scribner's Sons, 1990).

4. John C. Souter, "The Sky is Falling," *Future* (Wheaton, IL: Tyndale, 1984), 6.

5. Richard Erdoes, *AD 1000: Living on the Brink of Apocalypse* (San Francisco: Harper and Row, 1988), 1.

6. Souter, "Sky is Falling," 6.

7. J. F. C. Harrison, *The Second Coming: Popular Millennialism, 1780–1850* (New Brunswick, NJ: Rutgers University Press, 1979), 194. For a detailed description of Miller's views from a Seventh Day Adventist scholar, see LeRoy Edwin Froom, *The Prophetic Faith of Our Fathers: The Historical Development of Prophetic Interpretation*, 4 vols. (Washington, DC: Review and Herald, 1954), 4:429–876.

8. Harrison, *The Second Coming*, 195.

9. Ronald L. Numbers and Jonathan M. Butler, eds., "Introduction," *The Disappointed: Millerism and Millenarianism in the Nineteenth Century* (Bloomington, IN: Indiana University Press, 1987), xv.

10. Winthrop S. Hudson, *Religion in America: An Historical Account of the Development of American Religious Life* (New York: Charles Scribner's Sons, 1965), 364.

11. J. Marcellus Kik, *An Eschatology of Victory* (Nutley, NJ: Presbyterian and Reformed, 1975), 53–173.

12. Gary Friesen, "A Return Visit," *Moody Monthly* (May 1988), 30.

13. "Books with doomsday themes are selling well in Christian bookstores, thanks to current events in the Persian Gulf and fears that Saddam Hussein may drag the world into a fiery Armageddon. Zondervan Publishing House announced that sales of Hal Lindsey's 1970 multimillion seller 'The Late Great Planet Earth,' now in its 108th printing, shot up 83 percent between August and September [1990]. 'Often times we see during a crisis that people more actively turn toward God and things

spiritual,' Zondervan executive Paul Van Duinen said." (*National and International Religion Report* [October 22, 1990], 1).

14. Hal Lindsey, *The Late Great Planet Earth* (Grand Rapids, MI: Zondervan, [1970] 1971), 53–54.

15. Dean C. Halverson, "88 Reasons: What Went Wrong?," *Christian Research Journal* (Fall 1988), 17. For an interpretation of the fig tree illustration and the Olivet Discourse of Matthew 24, see Gary DeMar, *The Debate over Christian Reconstruction* (Ft. Worth, TX: Dominion Press, 1988), 143.

16. For a discussion of the various rapture positions, see Richard R. Reiter, et al., *The Rapture: Pre-, Mid-, or Post-Tribulational?* (Grand Rapids, MI: Zondervan/Acadamie, 1984).

17. Gary Wilburn, "The Doomsday Chic," *Christianity Today* (January 27, 1978), 22.

18. Hal Lindsey, *The 1980's: Countdown to Armageddon* (King of Prussia, PA: Westgate Press, 1980), 8. Emphasis in original.

19. Ibid., 31.

20. Ibid.

21. Ibid., 30.

22. W. Ward Gasque, "Future Fact? Future Fiction?," *Christianity Today* (April 15, 1977), 40.

23. Ibid.

24. Dale Moody, "The Eschatology of Hal Lindsey," *Review and Expositor* 72 (Summer 1975), 278.

25. In 1988 Edgar Whisenant predicted that the rapture would occur on September 12, 13, or 14 of that year (see Edgar Whisenant, *88 Reasons Why The Rapture Will Be in 1988* [Nashville, TN: World Bible Society, 1988]). As Whisenant admits in *The Final Shout: Rapture Report 1989*: "I was mistaken!" (p. 1). It seems that Whisenant made his calculations based on a faulty understanding of the calendar: "Since all centuries should begin with a zero (for instance, the year 1900 started this century), the first century A.D. was a year short, consisting of only 99 years. This was the one-year error in my calculations last year [1988]. The Gregorian calendar (the calendar used today) is always one year in advance of the true year." (Ibid.). Therefore, 1988 was actually 1987 while 1989 was 1988. Get it?

26. Chuck Smith, *Future Survival* (Costa Mesa, CA: Calvary Chapel, 1978), 20. Quoted in William M. Alnor, *Soothsayers of the Second Advent* (Old Tappan, NJ: Revell, 1989), 41.

27. Quoted in Alnor, *Soothsayers*, 41.

28. Friesen, "A Return Visit," 31.

29. George Eldon Ladd, *The Blessed Hope* (Grand Rapids, MI: Eerdmans, 1956), 106.

Chapter 15: "It's Never Right to Resist Authority"

1. Randy C. Alcorn, *Is Rescuing Right? Breaking the Law to Save the Unborn* (Downers Grove, IL: InterVarsity Press, 1990), 106.

2. John Jefferson Davis, *Evangelical Ethics: Issues Facing the Church Today* (Phillipsburg, NJ: Presbyterian and Reformed, 1985), 211.

3. Judge Randall Hekman, "Letter to the Editor," *Grand Rapids Press* (November 19, 1982). Quoted in Alcorn, *Is Rescuing Right?*, 79–80.

4. Alcorn, *Is Rescuing Right?*, 79.

5. John Murray, *Principles of Conduct: Aspects of Biblical Ethics* (London: The Tyndale Press, 1957), 139.

6. Gary North, "In Defense of Biblical Bribery," in Rousas J. Rushdoony, *The Institutes of Biblical Law* (Phillipsburg, NJ: Presbyterian and Reformed, 1973), 841.

7. Rushdoony, *Institutes*, 544.

8. Davis, *Evangelical Ethics*, 211–12.

9. Alcorn, *Is Rescuing Right?*, 104.

10. Tom Rose, "On Reconstruction and the American Republic," Gary North, ed. *Christianity and Civilization, The Theology of Christian Resistance* (Tyler, TX: Geneva Divinity School, 1983), 295–96.

11. Gene Fisher and Glen Chambers, *The Revolution Myth* (Greenville, SC: Bob Jones University Press, 1981), ix.

12. Ibid., ix-x.

13. Ibid., 62.

14. Norman L. Geisler, *Christian Ethics: Options and Issues* (Grand Rapids, MI: Baker Book House, 1989), 254.

15. Ibid., 237.

16. Jim West, "Rahab's Justifiable Lie," in *Christianity and Civilization: The Theology of Christian Resistance*, ed. Gary North (Tyler, TX: Geneva Divinity School Press, 1983), 68. Emphasis in original.

Conclusion

1. Robert Drake, "What Should the Kingdom of God Look Like?" A review of *Dominion Theology: Blessing or Curse?*, *World* (February 11, 1989).

2. Ibid.

3. Carl F. H. Henry, *Twilight of a Great Civilization: The Drift Toward Neo-Paganism* (Westchester, IL: Crossway Books, 1988), 30.

4. H. Wayne House, "Miscarriage or Premature Birth: Additional Thoughts on Exodus 21:22–25," *Westminster Theological Journal* 41(1) (Fall 1978), 108–123.

5. Our Western heritage, in the words of one social critic/historian, was "bequeathed by the Enlightenment." Anson Shupe, "Prophets of a Biblical America," *The Wall Street Journal* (April 12, 1989), 14A.

6. Francis A. Schaeffer, *How Should We Then Live?* in *The Complete Works of Francis A. Schaeffer*, 5 vols. (Westchester, IL: Crossway Books, 1982), 5:148.

7. Cotton Mather, *The Great Works of Christ in America*, 2 vols. (Edinburgh: The Banner of Truth Trust, [1702] 1979), 1:26.

8. Schaeffer, *How Should We Then Live?* in *The Complete Works of Francis Schaeffer*, 5:149.

9. Harold O. J. Brown, "Hidden Roots: Cultural Presuppositions of the Abortion Revolution," *The Human Life Review* 8(1) (Winter 1981), 69.

10. "Students Defend Abortion For 'High' Social Reasons," *The Rutherford Institute* 1(2) (January/February 1984), 8.

11. The following item appeared in *National and International Religion Report* (March 27, 1989):

> *Most Americans believe abortion is immoral, but they also think the choice* should be left to the woman, and they strongly oppose any constitutional amendments that would outlaw the procedure, a *Los Angeles Times* poll found. Although a large majority think abortion should be available in cases of incest, rape, and where the mother's life is endangered or a strong chance exists for serious birth defects, 61 percent said abortion is "morally wrong," and 57 percent classify it as "murder," the survey showed. Yet 74 percent said the choice should be left up to the woman. But 81 percent agreed minors should have parents' permission to obtain an abortion, and 53 percent said the natural father's consent should be required. Fully 60 percent said they firmly oppose a constitutional amendment to overturn the Supreme Court's Roe vs. Wade decision.

The poll shows that "57 percent classify" abortion "as murder," while 74 percent "said the choice should be left up to the woman." This means that a significant percentage believe that women should be permitted to commit murder.

12. Joseph Sobran, "The Non-Debate of 1988 Is on Abortion," *The Conservative Digest* (October 1988), 98.

SUBJECT INDEX

SCRIPTURE INDEX

ABOUT THE AUTHOR

G ary DeMar did his undergraduate work at Western Michigan University in 1973 and continued his education receiving a Master of Divinity degree at Reformed Theological Seminary in 1979. Since 1981, Gary has made his living as a writer and as president of American Vision, an Atlanta based educational ministry. He is also the editor of The Biblical Worldview and a popular lecturer.

Gary has written several books including the *God and Government* series and *Surviving College Successfully*, both published by Wolgemuth & Hyatt. He lives with his wife, Carol, and two sons, David and James, in Georgia.

The typeface for the text of this book is *Goudy Old Style*. Its creator, Frederic W. Goudy, was commissioned by American Type Founders Company to design a new Roman type face. Completed in 1915 and named Goudy Old Style, it was an instant bestseller. However, its designer had sold the design outright to the foundry, so when it became evident that additional versions would be needed to complete the family, the work was done by the foundry's own designer, Morris Benton. From the original design came seven additional weights and variants, all of which sold in great quantity. However, Goudy himself received no additional compensation for them. He later recounted a visit to the foundry with a group of printers, during which the guide stopped at one of the busy casting machines and stated, "Here's where Goudy goes down to posterity, while American Type Founders Company goes down to prosperity."

Substantive Editing:
Michael S. Hyatt

Copy Editing:
Karen Spear

Cover Design:
Steve Diggs & Friends
Nashville, Tennessee

Page Composition:
Xerox Ventura Publisher
Printware 720 IQ Laser Printer

Printing and Binding:
Maple-Vail Book Manufacturing Group,
York, Pennsylvania

Cover Printing:
Strine Printing Company
York, Pennsylvania